CONTEMPORARY'S

ESSENTIAL SKILLS FOR THE WORKPLACE
LEVEL TWO

Building Workplace Competencies

Series Developer
Lori Strumpf
President, Center for Remediation Design

Author
Kristine M. Mains

Project Editor
Cathy Niemet

CONTEMPORARY
BOOKS
CHICAGO

Library of Congress Cataloging-in-Publication Data

Strumpf, Lori.
    Essential skills for the workplace. Level two. Building workplace
competencies / Lori Strumpf, Kristine M. Mains.
        p.   cm.
    ISBN 0-8092-3902-7
    1. Office practice—Handbooks, manuals, etc.   2. Employees—
Training of—Handbooks, manuals, etc.   I. Mains, Kristine.
II. Title.   III. Title: Building workplace competencies.
HF5547.5.S8167   1993
651.3—dc20   93-39379
                                                   CIP

Published by Contemporary Books, Inc.
Two Prudential Plaza, Chicago, Illinois 60601-6790
Manufactured in the United States of America
International Standard Book Number: 0-8092-3902-7

10   9   8   7   6   5   4   3

Published simultaneously in Canada by
Fitzhenry & Whiteside
195 Allstate Parkway
Markham, Ontario L3R 4T8
Canada

Editorial Director
Mark Boone

Editorial
Joan McLaughlin
Leah Mayes
Lynn McEwan
Eunice Hoshizaki

Editorial Assistant
Maggie McCann

Editorial Production Manager
Norma Underwood

Production Editor
Jean Farley Brown

Cover Design
Georgene Sainati

Illustrator
Kathy Dzielak

Cover photo © Westlight
Photo manipulation by
    Kristin Nelson, Provizion

Art & Production
Jan Geist
Sue Springston

Typography
Point West, Inc.
Carol Stream, Illinois

Special thanks to
Caren Van Slyke

Acknowledgments: Charts on pages 25, 134, and 159
reprinted with permission from Inpatient Nursing, St.
John's Health System, Anderson, Indiana. Forms on
pages 88, 89, and 193 reprinted with permission from
The Worth Corporation.

Photo Credits: Page 5: © Don Klumpp/The Image Bank.
Page 6: © Sobel/Klonsky/The Image Bank. Page 19: ©
Jay Freis/The Image Bank. Page 20: © Michael Melford/
The Image Bank. Page 35: © Kay Chernush/The Image
Bank. Page 36: © Jay Freis/The Image Bank. Page 49:
© Romilly Lockyer/The Image Bank. Page 50: © Focus
International/The Image Bank. Page 67: © Lee
Balterman/FPG International. Page 68: © Art Montes de
Oca/FPG International. Page 83: © Arthur d'Arazien/
The Image Bank. Page 84: © Jay Freis/The Image Bank.
Page 99: © Morton Beebe/The Image Bank. Page 100:
© Wm. A. Logan/The Image Bank. Page 115: ©
Nickolay Zurek/FPG International. Page 116: ©
Schneps/The Image Bank.

Essential Skills for the Workplace stems from a national
demonstration project conducted by the Center for
Remediation Design (CRD), a joint project of the U.S.
Conference of Mayors, the National Association of
Private Industry Councils, the Partnership for Training
and Employment Careers, and the National Association
of Counties. The CRD's primary goal is to help
employers and training providers link basic skills
training to the needs of the workplace.

The Project of the States, conducted by the CRD, the
Center for Human Resources at Brandeis University,
and select JTPA entities since 1987, focuses on the use
of reading, writing, computation, problem solving, and
communication skills in the workplace. Competencies
singled out by this project's labor market studies as
being essential to a successful workforce are the
foundation for the lessons in this series.

CONTENTS

TO THE LEARNER

Contemporary's *Essential Skills for the Workplace* series has four books—two books in Level One, two books in Level Two. Each book integrates, or combines, the reading, math, writing, communication, and problem-solving skills you need to complete tasks at the workplace and in everyday life.

Essential Skills for the Workplace will take you out of the classroom and into the world of work. Each task in these books is a task you may encounter in the workplace. In addition, each task is part of the "big picture"—part of the process required to make a business purchase, for example, or to prepare a business delivery.

This book, *Building Workplace Competencies,* is part of Level Two of the series. In this book, you'll complete tasks you would perform in each of the eight career areas presented. The three units in each book are separated according to the level of difficulty. The tasks become more complex in Units II and III. When you finish the two workbooks in Level Two, you will have learned important skills needed to function well in the workplace.

In Level Two, you will

- ▶ visualize the steps you need to take to complete a task from start to finish
- ▶ prioritize tasks and do them in the order in which you would complete them
- ▶ make notes to help you organize your thoughts
- ▶ recap each task to check if you followed all the necessary steps
- ▶ review your plan to see if you might have done anything differently
- ▶ use the skills you've learned in your everyday life

Skills addressed in Level Two are

- ▶ selecting resources (time, money, space, and staff)
- ▶ gathering and interpreting information
- ▶ learning about organizational systems
- ▶ practicing interpersonal communication
- ▶ selecting technology and tools

In the back of the book, you'll find an answer key and a glossary of workplace terms. The words in boldface type throughout the book are the words defined in the glossary. You will also find several resource pages you'll need to complete the various workplace tasks.

We hope you enjoy *Essential Skills for the Workplace Level Two: Building Workplace Competencies.* We wish you the best of luck in your studies.

The Editors

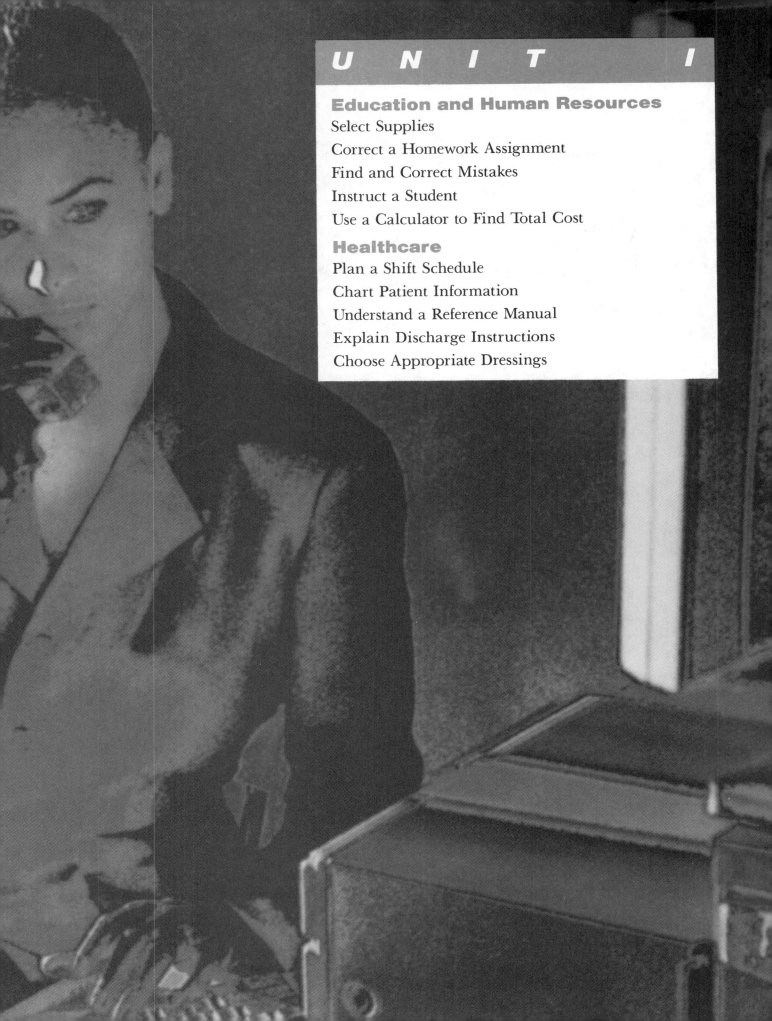

U N I T   I

Education and Human Resources

Select Supplies

Correct a Homework Assignment

Find and Correct Mistakes

Instruct a Student

Use a Calculator to Find Total Cost

Healthcare

Plan a Shift Schedule

Chart Patient Information

Understand a Reference Manual

Explain Discharge Instructions

Choose Appropriate Dressings

■■■ EDUCATION & HUMAN SERVICES

Compared to all jobs, the growth rate for education and human services jobs is expected to be much higher over the next 10 years. The rising U.S. population, increasing school enrollments, and growing number of elderly citizens lead to this job growth. Workers in this field deal with the physical and emotional needs of others. The work requires patience, the ability to motivate others, and some leadership and administrative abilities.

SOME SKILLS YOU WILL PRACTICE IN THIS LESSON

- ▶ Select Materials
- ▶ Evaluate and Interpret Information
- ▶ Monitor and Correct Performance
- ▶ Teach Others
- ▶ Apply Technology to Task

Teacher's aides are becoming very important in many schools. Because class size may be too large for one teacher to handle, teacher's aides can provide individual instruction and answer specific questions.

Teacher's aides may be responsible for planning entire lessons or developing parts of a lesson to meet the needs of an individual student. Because they may be responsible for correcting students' assignments, aides also correct and track students' progress.

If the need arises, teacher's aides may talk with parents about how they can encourage their children and explain how to participate in school activities.

SOME RELATED JOBS

childcare aide
GED instructor
teacher's assistant
employee trainer

One Teacher's Challenge

It's that time of year at Thomas Jefferson Junior High School when students are hustling to get papers and projects turned in, and teachers are bustling to grade those papers and projects to provide **feedback** to the students and their parents.

The class bell rings. A young boy is up and out the door before the instructor can say, "See you tomorrow." The students gather their belongings and race to their next class.

The last student darts quickly out the door as Felisha Williams, a fifth-grade teacher, says, "The end of the semester is always crazy. There's so much to do in so little time."

"Isn't that the truth? It seems like just as I finish one thing, I add two more to my list," you respond.

Frustrated, Felisha says, "I planned to get the supplies ordered for the special *Working with Percents* unit I planned, but I'm afraid with all of the parent

conferences coming up, I'm going to need your help with the ordering. I'll give you a supply list. Please **figure out what we need to order. Then use a calculator to find the total cost.**"

"No problem, Mrs. Williams, that's what I'm here for. I'll be ordering supplies for the *Decimals and Money* unit you asked me to plan, so I'll finish that today and **get both supply orders in.**"

"Thanks for the help. Speaking of help, **Tia Miles needs help** with adding two-digit decimals. Here's an idea I had to help her," Felisha says as she hands you some problems. She continues, "Would you work through the problems with her during her free work time at third period?"

"I'll make sure I work with her," you answer. "I also want to finish **correcting the rest of the assignments** from yesterday and **double-check the grade book** to make sure the students' grades have been recorded correctly." Smiling, you add, "Sounds like another busy day."

For the following lesson, you are a teacher's aide. The teacher, Felisha Williams, relies on you to help keep the children involved.

There are about 25 students in each class. Most of the time you work with fifth- and sixth-grade math students in Mrs. Williams's classroom. But, at the end of the semester, you may work with other teachers.

A teacher's aide has to jump from task to task in a matter of minutes. Think of this lesson as five tasks that you might perform in a given day. Each task is categorized as having to do with: resources, information, systems, interpersonal, and technology and tools.

SUMMARIZE THE TASKS

There are five tasks (highlighted in the story on page 6) that you will accomplish in this lesson. They are listed with the appropriate page number below.

CATEGORY	TASK	ORDER	PAGE
Resources	*select supplies for an activity*	____	8
Information	*correct a homework assignment*	____	10
Systems	*find and correct mistakes in the grade book*	____	12
Interpersonal	*instruct a student in a given area*	____	14
Technology and Tools	*use a calculator to find total cost* (*Hint:* You must do this task *after* you do *select supplies for an activity*.)	____	16

PLAN YOUR TIME

Think of this lesson as tasks done by a teacher's aide on a given day. You may need to do certain tasks before you can do others. In the ORDER column above, number the tasks in the order you would complete them.

The page order of the tasks in this workbook is not necessarily the order in which you would do them. Follow the order you decided above when you begin to work through the lesson.

THINK IT THROUGH

What will you need to do the tasks? • What resources? • What other information? • Are other people involved? It's OK if you need more information at this point. You will find more information as you work through each task.

Go to the task *you* listed as 1 and continue the lesson.

Resources: Teacher's aides must manage resources. One way they manage resources is by allocating, or selecting, the materials required.

SELECT SUPPLIES

Felisha has asked you to order supplies for a special fifth-grade activity, *Working with Percents.* At this time, you are deciding how much to order. Felisha has given you the following supply list. She has checked off the supplies she already has.

SUPPLIES

white poster boards (two per group)
black wide-tip markers (two per group)
green wide-tip markers (two per group)
✓ felt board (already have)
green felt squares (one for each student
✓ masking tape to hang finished poster boards (already have)
enough supplies for third period (25 students) and fourth
      period (28 students)

For this task you are to determine how many supplies you will need to order. According to her list, Felisha has designed this activity for groups. Usually, a group is five students. When there are more than 25 students, you add one extra student at a time to the five-person group.

For example, in fourth period there are 28 students:

$$5^{+1} + 5^{+1} + 5^{+1} + 5 + 5 = 28 \text{ students or 5 groups}$$

VISUALIZE THE WHOLE TASK

Visualizing is *seeing a picture in your mind.* Before you begin a task at work, you should picture it from beginning to end. Plan the steps you will take to complete the task.

Before you start the supply list, read back through the description above. Think through and write down the steps you will take to calculate how much material you will order. • What will you do first? • How much time do you think it will take you? • Do you need more information? • It's OK if you need more information at this point. You will find more information as you work through each task.

YOUR NOTES

How will you determine how many materials to order? Write down what steps you will take.

First, I will figure the number of groups for both classes. Then, I will start with the white

poster boards. Next, _____

_____

COMPLETE THE TASK

Use the supplies list on page 8 and the supply order worksheet to calculate the amount of supplies you will order for Felisha's *Working with Percents* group activity.

SUPPLY ORDER WORKSHEET THOMAS JEFFERSON JUNIOR HIGH		
Supply Description	**Notes**	**Total Amount**
white poster boards	10 groups x 2 boards = 20	20 white poster boards

TASK RECAP

▶ Did you write a complete description of the supplies you needed?
▶ Did you double-check your calculations?

REVIEW YOUR PLAN

Now that you've completed the supply order worksheet, what steps did you actually follow?

_____

_____

Information: One of the most important responsibilities of a teacher's aide is to provide feedback to a student. Feedback can be written (a graded assignment) or verbal (answering a question or saying "Good job").

CORRECT A HOMEWORK ASSIGNMENT

At the beginning of the day, you had several lessons, assignments, and projects to correct or grade. Now you are ready to correct the last assignment. The assignment belongs to Benita del Marco, a fifth-grade student. Benita has been told to show the numbers she carries at the top of each row when she adds numbers over 10.

For this task you will use the answer key on page 11 to grade Benita's assignment #9. Each problem is worth 3 points. If a student has the correct answer but has not shown the carrying, you take off 1 point.

Example   *Correct*

2.3   You would give 2 points for this answer. While it is correct,
13.7   Benita did not show the numbers she carried when she added.
+34.6
50.6

$$\begin{array}{r} \overset{1}{2}.3 \\ \overset{1}{1}3.7 \\ + 34.6 \\ \hline 50.6 \end{array}$$

The top of the answer key lists the chapter and lesson number of the homework. You could use a ruler or a small piece of paper to reveal one answer at a time on the answer key.

Next to each problem write +3 if Benita's answer is correct and she shows the numbers she carried, +2 if she forgot to show the numbers she carried, or 0 if the answer is incorrect.

When you have finished checking her answers:

1. Calculate her total points correct *(the maximum is 30)*.

2. Write the total points correct at the top of her homework assignment.

3. Write her total points correct in the grade book on page 12.

VISUALIZE THE WHOLE TASK

Before you start, think through the steps you will take to correct and record Benita's homework assignment. • What will you do first? • How much time do you think it will take you? • Do you need more information? • *Remember, it's OK if you need more information at this point. You will find more information as you work through the task.*

How will you correct and record Benita's homework assignment? What steps will you follow?

First, I will make sure her answer is correct. Then,

_____

_____

COMPLETE THE TASK

Use the answer key below to correct Benita's homework assignment. Then record her score for assignment #9 in the grade book on page 12.

Benita del Marco   Assignment #9
December 12

1. 2.3
   13.7
   + 34.6
   ———
   50.6

2. 12.37
   3.61
   + 14.28
   ———
   30.26

3. 2.316
   12.413
   + 3.714
   ———
   17.445

4. 3.4169
   2.2134
   + 3.4192
   ———
   9.0495

5. 11.3
   12.6
   48.0
   + 29.6
   ———
   101.5

6. 7.14
   2.47
   36.72
   + 84.92
   ———
   131.25

7. 4.702
   46.843
   18.937
   9.247
   + 83.201
   ———
   162.930

8. 7.4136
   8.2004
   9.3090
   6.6748
   + 5.9216
   ———
   37.5194

9. 837.42
   84.24
   2.1
   + 176.837
   ———
   1100.597

10. 9.2
    11.03
    23.476
    + 37.0009
    ———
    70.7069

Answer Key
Chapter 4
Assignment #9
1. 50.6
2. 30.26
3. 18.443
4. 9.0495
5. 101.5
6. 131.25
7. 162.930
8. 37.5194
9. 1100.597
10. 80.7069

TASK RECAP

▶ Did you write the total correct at the top of Benita's homework assignment?
▶ Did you record Benita's score in the grade book under assignment #9 on page 12?

REVIEW YOUR PLAN

Now that you have corrected, totaled, and recorded Benita's assignment, look at your plan. • What steps did you actually follow?

_____

_____

Systems: Teachers and teacher's aides use grade books to keep track of students' performance. Grade books may be organized by *class* (fifth grade), *period* (third hour class), or even by *individual student*. Because each teacher uses his or her own system of grading, you need to become familiar with various grading systems so that you can recognize and fix mistakes.

FIND AND CORRECT MISTAKES

Felisha used this system for grading her students' homework assignments. First, she wrote the grade number of the class. Then, at the top of each row, she wrote the total points possible for each homework assignment and under that the assignment number. Next, she wrote the students' names in alphabetical order and entered the scores for the students' homework assignments. Finally, she added the scores for the individual assignments to get the total score for each student.

Sometimes teachers make mistakes when they have several class periods a day with a lot of students in each class and not much time to correct and grade students' homework assignments.

For this task you will be double-checking to see if Felisha's total scores are correct for each student.

GRADE BOOK

5th Grade NAME	#1 20 pts.	#2 25 pts.	#3 30 pts.	#4 100 pts.	#5 30 pts.	#6 30 pts.	#7 100 pts.	#8 25 pts.	#9 30 pts.	#10 100 pts.	490 pts.
E. Alexander	18	24	30	96	25	28	92	24	27	94	468
D. Brown	19	25	30	98	29	29	97	24	30	98	479
J. Catron	15	21	28	86	21	20	74	23	24	80	382
K. Dellinger	11	14	20	65	18	19	64	18	21	68	318
B. del Marco	18	20	27	94	24	28	91	22		93	
E. Estevez	20	25	29	98	30	28	99	24	30	99	464
A. Fontana	12	0	15	71	17	18	76	0	19	73	301
S. Groebel	17	22	26	88	26	25	85	24	27	90	430

Before you start, think through the steps you will take to correct the grade book. • What will you do first? • How much time do you think it will take you? • Do you need more information?

YOUR NOTES

How will you find mistakes in the total score? What tool might be helpful?

I will use a calculator to _____

_____

_____

COMPLETE THE TASK

In the grade book on page 12, find and correct any mistakes in each student's total score. Cross out the incorrect score and write the correct score next to it. Find Benita's total score by adding her scores together. You may want to use a calculator to check and re-check your answers.

TASK RECAP

▶ Did you add the total for all 10 lessons for each student?
▶ Did you check to make sure your total was less than 490 points?
▶ Did you find the incorrect total score and write the correct score next to it?

REVIEW YOUR PLAN

Look at page 132, where you will find the corrections you should have made. • What did you do differently than you had planned?

_____

_____

_____

Interpersonal: On the job, you may need to train co-workers (a form of teaching). Part of a teacher's aide's job is to **tutor** and **encourage** students so that they do their best.

INSTRUCT A STUDENT

"Tia, I saw you practicing your math yesterday. You are so persistent," Rosie Odell praised.

"Ms. Odell, I just can't get it. I keep forgetting something," explains Tia Miles, a fifth-grade math student.

"You'll get it. Let me show you a trick. Draw a line like this," Rosie instructs as she draws a line from the top to the bottom of her paper. She continues, "Every time you add decimals you line up the decimal point right on the line. OK? Now, let's try another one together."

"OK, Ms. Odell," responds Tia, "I'll try, but only if you help me again."

"That's what I'm here for," smiles Rosie.

For this task you will actually practice instructing another person. You will also think of two positive comments you might make to a student who says, "I can't do it."

You may ask a classmate, your husband, wife, child, or friend to be your student.

At the beginning of this lesson, you read that Tia Miles needed help with adding decimals. Mrs. Williams, a teacher, gave Rosie a **tutoring aid** (page 15) that she wanted her to use in instructing Tia.

Felisha explained, "Have Tia trace the vertical line before she begins each problem. That will help her remember to line up the decimals before she starts adding."

Reread the dialogue shown above between Rosie Odell and Tia. What positive remark did Rosie make to Tia?

"Tia, I saw you practicing your math yesterday. You are so persistent," Rosie Odell praised.

Rosie noted something positive about Tia's work and praised her for being "persistent." When you write a positive statement:

▶ *keep it simple*—"I'm glad you're here today."
▶ *focus on something positive*—"You have one more correct."
▶ *make it a team effort*—"Let's try another one together."

Think through the steps you will take to practice teaching a student. • Who will you teach? • What questions might the student ask? • How can you be prepared? • What resources do you need? • What will you do first? • How long do you think it will take? • Do you need more information?

YOUR NOTES
How will you arrange the teaching session? Who will be your student? How much time will it take? What positive approach statement can you write for your student? *I like the way you* _____ _____

COMPLETE THE TASK

Using the positive approach statement you wrote, and the decimal addition problems on the tutoring aid shown at the right (with the vertical lines drawn down through the periods), practice teaching a student how to do the problems. Your student could be a classmate, teacher, friend, or family member.

Add the following decimals.		
1.3 + 2.6	54.29 + 22.72	9.363 + .759
4.1 + 5.9	36.50 + 80.47	1.888 + 3.294
6.2 + 1.7	62.60 + 57.60	7.237 + 5.193

TASK RECAP

► Did you start with a positive approach statement?
► Did you have the student trace the vertical lines before adding the decimals?

REVIEW YOUR PLAN

How did you do? Ask your student how he or she felt. • Did the person feel you communicated clearly? • Were you organized? • Were you positive?

_____

_____

_____

Technology and Tools: Many teachers and teacher's aides use computers, calculators, and other equipment on their jobs. For example, calculators make it much easier to average test scores, calculate grades, figure budgets, and create answer keys.

USE A CALCULATOR TO FIND TOTAL COST

For this task you will need to use a calculator. Remember this supply list? You will price or find the cost of each item needed.

SUPPLIES

white poster boards (two per group) $.50/board
black wide-tip markers (two per group) $1.19/marker
green wide-tip markers (two per group) $1.19/marker
✓ felt board (already have)
green felt squares (one for each student) $.29/square
✓ masking tape to hang finished poster boards (already have)
enough supplies for third period (25 students) and fourth
     period (28 students)

VISUALIZE THE WHOLE TASK

Before you start, think through the steps you will take to calculate how much your supplies will cost. • What will you do first? • How much time do you think it will take? • Do you need more information? Materials?

How do you calculate the cost of each supply? (*Hint:* quantity × cost) How will you calculate the total supply cost? What step will you do first? Second?

YOUR NOTES

First, I will _____

_____

_____

_____

_____

Using the supply order worksheet on page 9, finish the order form below. Calculate the total cost of the supplies. First, look up the quantity of each item you found on page 9. Then, multiply the quantity by the unit cost to get the total. Then, add your totals together to get your total cost.

ORDER FORM			
Quantity	**Product**	**Unit Price**	**Total**
20	white poster boards	.50	10.00

TASK RECAP

▶ Did you transfer the complete supply description and quantity?

▶ Did you calculate each supply total?

▶ Did you remember to clear the calculator before you started a new calculation?

▶ Did you double-check your calculations?

Now that you've completed the supply order form and totaled the supply costs, what steps did you actually follow?

_____

_____

_____

Is your total the same as the one on page 132? What's different about your order?

_____

_____

USE WHAT YOU'VE LEARNED

You have been learning a variety of skills within the context of being a teacher's aide. Some of these skills are

- ▶ managing resources
- ▶ interpreting information
- ▶ budgeting
- ▶ oral communication
- ▶ scanning for information
- ▶ visualizing a whole task

Although the skills listed above related to the work of a teacher's aide in this lesson, you might use the same type of skills on other jobs. When you learn skills for one job and use those skills on another job, those skills are called *transferable skills*.

1. Name two other jobs that might require these skills. How might these skills be put to use?

   Example: *an accountant helps a client understand an item on a tax form*
   _____

   _____

   _____

   _____

2. Is there anywhere else you've used these skills? Where?

   Example: *I scanned a table of contents to find out what a book was about*
   _____

   _____

   _____

   _____

3. Now that you have completed the tasks in this lesson, can you think of two new tasks at work or at home that you might try? What are they?

   _____

   _____

   _____

   _____

■■■ HEALTHCARE

The healthcare industry is one of the fastest-growing fields in the United States. Nearly 4 million jobs are expected to open in the health services industry by the year 2005. More and more health service workers will be needed to care for the growing number of elderly Americans. Advances in medical technology also require more workers in new types of health services. Workers in this field care for others. They help people improve their physical well-being.

SOME SKILLS YOU WILL PRACTICE IN THIS LESSON

► Allocate Time
► Interpret and Communicate Information
► Understand Systems
► Serve Patients
► Select Technology

One job in the healthcare field is licensed practical nurse (LPN). LPNs provide bedside care to patients with a variety of needs. LPNs work in doctors' offices, nursing homes, hospitals, medical clinics, and private homes.

Depending on the organization, LPNs perform a wide variety of both clinical nursing and clerical tasks. LPNs' clinical responsibilities include taking temperatures, pulse, blood pressure; observing and reporting a patient's activities or requests; administering medications as prescribed; and other bedside care—giving patients bed baths or lifting patients from bed to chair.

LPNs' clerical responsibilities include recording patient information on a variety of forms, planning schedules, and entering patient information into a data base on a computer.

SOME RELATED JOBS

medical assistant
home health aide
medical technologist
registered nurse
dental hygienist
physician's assistant

Life on 5 South

You've arrived 15 minutes early at the hospital. You see the "5" light up on the panel and hear the ding of the elevator. As the steel doors of the service elevator open, you hear a familiar voice saying, "It's all right, Mr. Bower. We're going down to x-ray to see what's going on in that chest of yours."

As you exchange winks and smiles, James, a transportation aide, **maneuvers** Mr. Bower in his wheelchair to the back of the elevator. Mr. Bower grumbles something under his breath as you turn toward the hallway.

As you enter the east main hall, you can see some patients are already awakened.

Your unit practices a team-care approach. The team is made up of a registered nurse (RN), an LPN, and a nursing assistant. In the staff room you find Meg Samuels, the RN of your team, looking over the patient status report. "Looks like we have five beds today. Mrs. de Vecchio is going home today."

Meg hands you the report and adds, "It looks like I'll need help changing Mr. Mundorf's dressings today. It should take 15 extra minutes at the most. I'll go get the patient files for our meeting."

You begin your shift with a team meeting during which you assign the day's tasks and **plan your shift schedule**. Once you've completed your schedule, you begin reviewing the charts of your five patients.

In Room 362, Mrs. de Vecchio is being discharged this morning. You usually allow an extra 30 minutes to **complete a referral form to Social Services** and **explain follow-up instructions to patients.** You will need to **chart your observations and any activity of Mrs. de Vecchio.**

Mr. Mundorf has dressings (bandages) that will require an additional 15-minute visit in the afternoon. You will **decide what tools are appropriate**, or needed, for changing dressings.

The remaining four patients should only require routine 15-minute consultations.

The rest of the time on your schedule is left open for:

• answering patient calls

• completing paperwork

• doctor consultations

• lunch and breaks

An LPN has to maintain a **flexible** schedule to allow enough time to work with each patient and chart, or record, patient activity. You will complete five specific tasks in this lesson. Each task is categorized as having to do with one of the following: resources, information, systems, interpersonal, and technology and tools.

SUMMARIZE THE TASKS

There are five tasks (highlighted in the story on page 20) that you will accomplish in this lesson. They have been listed for you below. The page number on which each task is taught is also listed.

CATEGORY	TASK	ORDER	PAGE
Resources	*plan a shift schedule*	____	22
Information	*chart observations and patient activity*	____	24
Systems	*understand how to complete a referral form*	____	26
Interpersonal	*explain discharge instructions*	____	28
Technology and Tools	*choose appropriate dressing materials*	____	30

PLAN YOUR TIME

Think of this lesson as tasks done by an LPN on a given day. You may need to do certain tasks before you can do others. In the ORDER column above, number the tasks 1 through 5 in the order you would complete them.

Hint: Plan _____ . Write 1 in the ORDER column above.

The page order of the tasks in this workbook is not necessarily the order in which you would do them. Follow the order that you decided above when you begin to work through the lesson.

THINK IT THROUGH

What will you need to do the tasks? • What resources? • What other information? • How much time will it take to complete each task? • To complete all the tasks?

▶ Now go on to the task *you* listed as 1 and continue the lesson.

Resources: Allocating time in scheduling is one key element to successful care giving. As an LPN, scheduling and rescheduling your time will help you be organized, prevent duplication of services, and save staff time in the long run.

PLAN A SHIFT SCHEDULE

Because an LPN may perform both clinical nursing and clerical duties, **prioritizing** tasks and allocating time for tasks may vary. **For this task, you are on 5 South, the unit described in the narrative on page 20. Plan a shift schedule, considering the following amounts of time you need to complete various tasks.**

- ▶ 15 minutes *average* per patient consultation (visit)
- ▶ 10 minutes *average* to complete each patient's chart
- ▶ Lunch hour from 12:00 to 1:00 P.M.
- ▶ 15-minute morning break
- ▶ 15-minute afternoon break
- ▶ Two 15-minute team meetings (at the beginning and end of each shift)

Your supervisor has given you the following team assignment sheet:

RN _Samuels, Meg_ LPN _____ (your name)	NA _Jansen, Pam_
Patient	Room #
Adams, Thomas B.	355
deVecchio, Angelina M.	362
Lichens, Marie L.	368
Mundorf, Donald J.	350
Sheehan, Evan A.	352

You always give a copy of your shift schedule to the unit clerk so that you can be located easily. *You may want to include where you will be during each activity.*

VISUALIZE THE WHOLE TASK

Before you start planning your shift schedule, think through the steps you will take. • What will you do first? • How much time do you think it will take? • What other information do you need? • Who is involved?

```
┌─────────────────────────────────────────────────────────┐
│                      YOUR NOTES                           │
├─────────────────────────────────────────────────────────┤
│  Which activity will you do first? Second? Third? Write  │
│  down the steps you will follow to plan your day's       │
│  schedule.                                                │
│                                                           │
│  First, I will _____     │
│                                                           │
│  _____        │
│                                                           │
│  _____        │
│                                                           │
└─────────────────────────────────────────────────────────┘
```

COMPLETE THE TASK

Using the shift schedule form on page 157, plan your day's scheduled activities. List the specific time when you will see each patient, write in each patient's chart, eat lunch, and take your two breaks.

TASK RECAP

▶ Did you allow the **appropriate** amount of time for each activity, including the extra time needed for completing the patients' charts?

▶ Did you include each patient's name and room number?

REVIEW YOUR PLAN

Now that you've filled out the shift schedule, what steps did you actually follow?

_____

_____

_____

• Does your completed shift schedule look something like the sample on page 133?

• What is different about your schedule?

_____

_____

_____

Information: Charting patient information is a kind of written communication that forms an important link in exchanging patient information.

CHART PATIENT INFORMATION

As an LPN, one of your key responsibilities is to chart your observations about patients and their activities. 5 South uses several forms that serve a variety of purposes.

For this task you will record a patient's vital information on a patient summary record (PSR) and a patient's responses and requests for medication on a patient progress record (PPR).

Before you can chart information about your patient, you have a consultation with her.

Patient Consultation: 10/20/93, 11:00 A.M.

Mrs. de Vecchio says, "I started feeling the pain again in my leg about two hours after you gave me my pain medicine."

You ask her, "On a scale of 1 to 10, how bad is your pain?"

"A 7. It hurts awfully bad. Can't you give me more medicine?" pleads Mrs. de Vecchio.

You assure her, saying, "I'll ask the doctor what we can do for you."

VISUALIZE THE WHOLE TASK

Think about the steps you will follow before you chart your observations. • What will you do first? • What materials will you use? • Do you need other information?

YOUR NOTES

How will you know what information you will need to chart the patient information? Which patient records do you need? Write down the steps you will take.

_____

_____

Step 1 Chart your patient's vital signs. The first reading is labeled for you. Chart the patient's last three readings (4, 5, and 6) on the PSR chart below.

PSR Chart

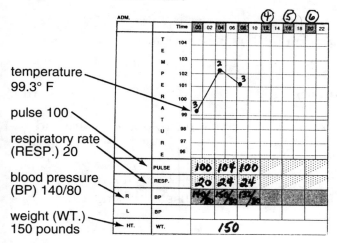

temperature
99.3° F

pulse 100

respiratory rate
(RESP.) 20

blood pressure
(BP) 140/80

weight (WT.)
150 pounds

Reading	Temp.	Pulse	Resp.	BP
4	100.1	92	20	132/80
5	100.4	112	20	150/84
6	100.6	112	20	130/82

Step 2 Reread your patient consultation with Mrs. de Vecchio on page 24. Record your observations on the patient progress record (PPR) on page 159. Write the date and time of observation and the patient's comments about pain and needing more medication. For example:

Date	Hour	Code	Notations
10/20/93	0900	N	Morphine 2 mg given in IVP for pain in lower left leg for pain and abdominal discomfort.

TASK RECAP

▶ Did you record your patient's vital signs on the PSR chart?
▶ Did you include the date, hour, code, and appropriate notations about your patient's medication and comments she made about her condition?

Now that you have charted the patient information on the PPR and the PSR, what steps did you actually follow?

_____

_____

Systems: Each hospital, doctor's office, or nursing home has many systems. Documentation, or paperwork, is used to track how something or someone moves through a system. As a healthcare professional, you should know which departments provide what services and how patients are referred to those services.

UNDERSTAND A REFERENCE MANUAL

For this task you will complete a referral form for Mrs. de Vecchio.

To know the specific services of the Social Services Department and its referral procedures, see the reference manual on page 159.

Yesterday, while you were checking Mrs. de Vecchio's vital signs (blood pressure and heart rate), she said:

> "Since Giuseppe died, I don't cook anymore. I don't feel like eating. I'm tired of being alone and cooking for myself. What's the use in cooking a meal if nobody's around to enjoy it?"

After charting your observations, you talked to the doctor and asked if a Social Services referral was appropriate. The doctor wrote this note in Mrs. de Vecchio's chart:

DATE	NOTES SHOULD BE SIGNED BY PHYSICIAN
11-2	Pt. is to be discharged 11-3. Refer to Social Services Dept. for assessment of Life Management (60 days) and Home Hospice Care Program for Nutrition. *Gregory Lambert, MD*

VISUALIZE THE WHOLE TASK

Before you complete a referral form, think through the steps you will follow.
• What will you do first? • How long will it take to locate the appropriate services?
• How many services does the patient need?

YOUR NOTES
How will you make the appropriate referral for Mrs. de Vecchio? What steps will you follow to ensure that she is referred to the proper services?
First, I will _____
_____
_____

According to the doctor's note on page 26, which two services should be provided for Mrs. de Vecchio?

_____   _____

Complete the referral form below only for the home hospice care needed by your patient, Angelina de Vecchio. See the Social Services Department listing on page 159 for the correct referral information.

DISCHARGE INSTRUCTIONS	INSTRUCTION CARD GIVEN
Follow laceration instruction card. Keep clean and dry. Salve tonight. Take Advil for pain. REFERRED TO Name _____ Address _____ _____ Contact _____ Phone _____ Physician _____ Nurse _____ Nurse's Aide _____	☐ CAST CARE ☐ CRUTCH WALKING ☐ SPRAINS/SOFT TISSUE ☐ COLDS/SORE THROAT ☐ VOMITING/DIARRHEA ☐ URINARY TRACT INFECTION ☐ HERPES ☐ GONORRHEA ☐ PREG/VAG. BLEEDING ☐ LACERATION ☐ EYE INJURY ☐ ANIMAL BITE ☐ FEVER ☐ HEAD INJURY ☐ CHEST PAIN ☐ LOWER BACK INJURY ☐ OTHER

Patient Name	EU Number	Physician	Date
	E-284682		

TASK RECAP

▶ Did you list the appropriate services to which Mrs. de Vecchio was referred?
▶ Did you sign and date the referral form?
▶ Did you check the Social Services reference manual listing?

Now that you have completed the referral form, look at your plan. • What steps did you actually follow? • What did you do differently?

_____

_____

Interpersonal: Working with patients is a care giver's primary responsibility. Nurse's aides are often responsible for patient education. They teach patients about self-care, surgical procedures, and medications so that patients understand their illnesses.

EXPLAIN DISCHARGE INSTRUCTIONS

Mrs. de Vecchio is going home from the hospital today. She had a hip replacement three weeks ago. It was decided in your team meeting this morning that you are responsible for explaining Mrs. de Vecchio's discharge instructions to her.

For this task you will practice instructing a patient. (Ask another student, co-worker, friend, or family member to act as your patient.) Reread the physician's notes below and discharge instructions you completed on page 27.

DATE	NOTES SHOULD BE SIGNED BY PHYSICIAN
11-2	Pt. is to be discharged 11-3. Refer to Social Services Dept. for assessment of Life Management (60 days) and Home Hospice Care Program for Nutrition. _Gregory Lambert, MD_

DISCHARGE INSTRUCTIONS	INSTRUCTION CARD GIVEN			
Follow laceration instruction card. Keep clean and dry. Salve tonight. Take Advil for pain. REFERRED TO Name _____ Address _____ _____ Contact _____ Phone _____ Physician _____ Nurse _____ Nurse's Aide _____	☐ CAST CARE ☐ CRUTCH WALKING ☐ SPRAINS/SOFT TISSUE ☐ COLDS/SORE THROAT ☐ VOMITING/DIARRHEA ☐ URINARY TRACT INFECTION ☐ HERPES ☐ GONORRHEA ☐ PREG/VAG. BLEEDING ☐ LACERATION ☐ EYE INJURY ☐ ANIMAL BITE ☐ FEVER ☐ HEAD INJURY ☐ CHEST PAIN ☐ LOWER BACK INJURY ☐ OTHER			
Patient Name	**EU Number**		**Physician**	**Date**
	E-284682			

Think through the steps you will take to instruct your patient. • How will you arrange the patient education session? • How much time will it take? • What resources will you need to explain the discharge instructions?

YOUR NOTES
What will you explain first? Second? Third? How long do you think it will take? Write down the steps you will follow.

_____

_____

_____

COMPLETE THE TASK

Reread the script on page 24 to become familiar with your patient's physical problems and complaints about pain. Then explain the physician's notes and discharge instructions on page 28 telling your patient about the referrals the doctor has made.

TASK RECAP

► Did you help your patient feel comfortable about leaving the hospital?
► Did you explain the physician's notes, referrals, and discharge instructions in a way your patient could understand them?

REVIEW YOUR PLAN

How did you do? • Did your patient feel at ease? • Did your patient understand your instructions? • Did your patient feel you communicated clearly? • What steps did you actually follow?

_____

_____

_____

• What would you do or say differently?

_____

_____

Technology and Tools: In the medical profession, because of the advancement in technology, you are continually trained and retrained about how to select the tools and instruments you use in your daily work. One way to learn how to use these updated instruments is by observing other professionals.

CHOOSE APPROPRIATE DRESSINGS

For this task you will need to get permission to observe an LPN changing a dressing, or bandage.

▶ Call a hospital, nursing home, or doctor's office and explain that you would like to observe an LPN working with a patient. *You will want to prepare what you are going to say before you call.*

▶ Complete this lesson and make any additional notes about your experience. Use the following questions as a guide when you talk to the LPN.

OBSERVATION CHECKLIST

▶ Where does the LPN work?
▶ Where did the LPN learn how to change dressings?
▶ What types of dressings does the LPN change?
▶ Has the LPN received additional training?
▶ How does the LPN choose instruments and materials?
▶ What procedure manuals does the LPN use?
▶ What type of training does an LPN need?

VISUALIZE THE WHOLE TASK

Before you start, think through the steps you will take to set up and complete your observation. • What will you do first? • Who will you call? • How much time do you think it will take? • How will you get there? • Do you need more information? • What other people are involved?

YOUR NOTES
How will you set up your appointment? What steps will you follow to complete your observation?
_____
_____
_____
_____

Use the observation checklist on page 30 as a guide when you go to observe an LPN at work and talk about dressings, instruments, and background needed for the job.

TASK RECAP

▶ Did you complete the checklist?

▶ Were you able to identify the tools and materials after observing the LPN?

▶ Did you thank the appropriate people with a handwritten thank-you note?

REVIEW YOUR PLAN

Now that you've completed your observation and checklist, what steps did you actually follow?

_____

_____

_____

_____

• What additional information did you learn about the job of an LPN? • What did you learn about changing dressings?

_____

_____

_____

_____

_____

_____

_____

_____

_____

_____

_____

USE WHAT YOU'VE LEARNED

In this lesson you have been learning various skills within the context of a day in the life of a licensed practical nurse (LPN). Some of these skills are

▶ allocating time for specific tasks
▶ using good judgment
▶ prioritizing information
▶ communicating verbally
▶ summarizing information

1. Name two other jobs that might require these skills. How might these skills be put to use?

2. Is there anywhere else you've used these skills? Where?

3. Now that you've completed this lesson, can you think of two new tasks that you might try at work or at home? What are they?

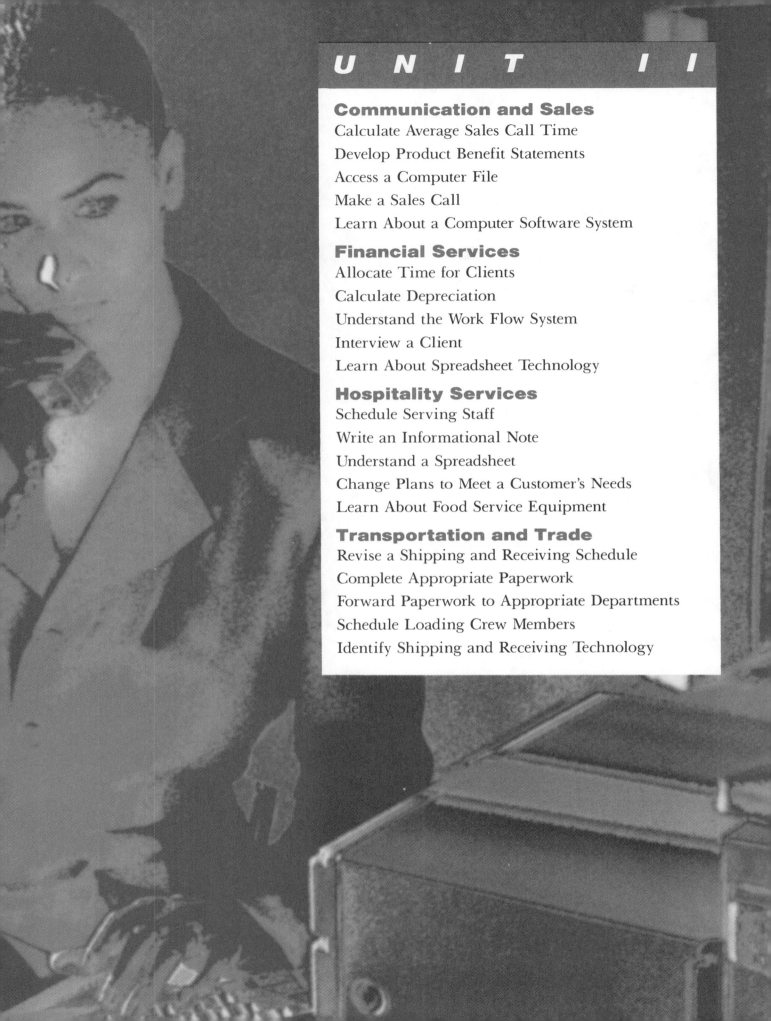

U N I T   I I

Communication and Sales
Calculate Average Sales Call Time
Develop Product Benefit Statements
Access a Computer File
Make a Sales Call
Learn About a Computer Software System

Financial Services
Allocate Time for Clients
Calculate Depreciation
Understand the Work Flow System
Interview a Client
Learn About Spreadsheet Technology

Hospitality Services
Schedule Serving Staff
Write an Informational Note
Understand a Spreadsheet
Change Plans to Meet a Customer's Needs
Learn About Food Service Equipment

Transportation and Trade
Revise a Shipping and Receiving Schedule
Complete Appropriate Paperwork
Forward Paperwork to Appropriate Departments
Schedule Loading Crew Members
Identify Shipping and Receiving Technology

■■■COMMUNICATION AND SALES

The growth rate for jobs in the communication and sales field is expected to be about the same as that for all jobs. This growth depends on the growth of the retail and service industries. Workers in this field deal with the public almost constantly. They provide a variety of services such as waiting on customers and accepting payment for purchases or services.

SOME SKILLS YOU WILL PRACTICE IN THIS LESSON

▶ Allocate Time
▶ Develop Product Benefit Statements
▶ Access a Computer File
▶ Negotiate During a Sales Call
▶ Learn About a Computer Software System

You may have received a telephone call from a telemarketing **representative** before. Companies use telemarketing reps to gain quick access to customers at home or at work. Telemarketing reps make market research calls.

For a company's existing customers, telemarketing reps may handle credit problems, billing questions, account upgrades, or accounting cancellations. Telemarketing reps may ask questions about products or services people buy. Telemarketing reps may ask what laundry detergent people buy, what long-distance company they use, what kind of car they own, or whether they've used a certain product.

SOME RELATED JOBS

travel agent
retail salesperson
account executive
customer service rep

A Telephone Call Away

It's telemarketing blitz day, the day when you make sales calls to potential customers.

You have spent the previous two days **calculating average sales call time, developing your product benefit statements**, and **learning about your new computer software. Accessing your first customer file from your qualified computer file, you make the first call**.

"Hello?" answers Mr. Osgoode.

"Good morning. Is Mr. Osgoode there?" you ask.

"This is Mr. Osgoode."

"Mr. Osgoode, this is _____ with Power Mowers Unlimited. I'm calling homeowners in your area to see how we can best meet their needs. It'll only take a moment. Do you mind telling me whether you presently own a riding lawn mower?"

"Well, yes we do," says Mr. Osgoode.

"Oh, fine." Right away, you add, "May I ask what type and make it is?"

"Let's see. We bought it 10 years ago. It's an older John Deere. May I ask what this is for?"

"Sure, Mr. Osgoode. At Power Mowers Unlimited we carry various kinds of lawn equipment, including riding mowers like the John Deere you currently own. What do you like most about your current riding mower?"

At this point, the call could go many

ways. Mr. Osgoode is friendly, so you continue to discuss his riding mower with him. You feel he might be interested in buying a new riding mower.

You work to set up an appointment for Mr. Osgoode to talk with a sales agent—your ultimate goal. You ask, "Would two o'clock be the best time for you?"

"Well, that'd be fine," adds Mr. Osgoode.

"I have your current address as 304 River View Circle. Is that correct?"

"That's right," says Mr. Osgoode.

"According to the service schedule, Devon Myer will be the agent in your area at two o'clock. Thank you for talking with me today," you continue.

"Well, you're welcome, _____."

"Have a nice day, Mr. Osgoode."

A telemarketing representative must complete several tasks in order to make a sale or compile information. Think of this lesson as five tasks you might perform as a telemarketing rep. No matter what the purpose of the call, as a telemarketing rep must:

▶ introduce yourself and the name of the company
▶ always be courteous with every call
▶ never lose your temper

SUMMARIZE THE TASKS

There are five tasks (highlighted in the story on page 36) that you will accomplish in this lesson. They are listed with the appropriate page number below. Reread the story on page 36 to find each of them.

CATEGORY	TASK	ORDER	PAGE
Resources	*calculate average sales call time*	____	38
Information	*develop a product benefit statement*	____	40
Systems	*access a computer file*	____	42
Interpersonal	*make a sales call*	____	44
Technology and Tools	*learn about computer software*	____	46

PLAN YOUR TIME

Think of this lesson as five tasks a telemarketing rep may perform in a week. You may need to do certain tasks before you can do others. In the ORDER column above, number the tasks in the order you would complete them.

The page order of the tasks in this workbook is not necessarily the order in which you would do them. Follow the order that you decided above when you begin to work through the lesson.

THINK IT THROUGH

What will you need to do the tasks? • What resources? • What other information? • Are other people involved?

Go to the task *you* listed above as 1 and continue the lesson.

Resources: Telemarketing representatives are usually working under a time pressure of some kind. Setting sales goals and calculating average sales call time are two ways a telemarketing rep may allocate time.

CALCULATE AVERAGE SALES CALL TIME

Telemarketing reps may make both random and qualified telephone sales calls. In the story on page 36, you used a qualified list of potential customers.

In this case, the qualified list includes customers who have:

▶ purchased the same type of product as the telemarketing rep is selling
▶ purchased a similar type of product
▶ inquired about the same or similar product by telephone, in writing, or in person
▶ reported problems with the same type of product

The more calls or contacts you have with qualified customers, the more appointments and sales you can make.

For this task you will calculate the average sales call time it takes to make this sales goal. Your sales goal is one sale per hour for three different products. You'll use this list:

Average number of sales per hour made from sales calls

▶ Product A: 6 qualified calls/hour → 3 appointments → 1 sale
▶ Product B: 5 qualified calls/hour → 2 appointments → 1 sale
▶ Product C: 10 qualified calls/hour → 4 appointments → 1 sale

To calculate your *average sales call time* for Product A, follow this formula:

One hour ÷ number of qualified calls = average sales call time

60 minutes ÷ 6 qualified calls = 10 minutes per sales call

VISUALIZE THE WHOLE TASK

Visualizing is *seeing a picture in your mind.* Before you calculate your average sales call time for Products B and C, read back through the description above. Think through and write down the steps you will allocate to each sales call. • What will you do first? • How much time will it take you? • Do you need more information?

YOUR NOTES
How will you calculate your average sales call time? Write down what steps you will take.
First, I will copy onto a piece of paper the equation: One hour ÷ number of qualified calls = average sales call time (in minutes). Then, I will _____

COMPLETE THE TASK

Use a separate sheet of paper and determine the average sales call time for Products B and C. Complete the daily activity goals sheet below. Fill in the *Goal* and the *Avg. Call* columns for all three products.

DAILY ACTIVITY GOALS

ACTIVITY	SALES GOAL	AVG. CALL (mins.)
Product "A"	1 per hour	10 minutes/call
Product "B"		
Product "C"		

TASK RECAP

▶ Did you calculate the daily goals for all three products?
▶ Did you write the amount of minutes needed for an average call?

REVIEW YOUR PLAN

Now that you've calculated the average sales call time and completed the Daily Activity Goals for Products A, B, and C, what steps did you actually follow? • What tools, resources, or information did you use?

_____

_____

Information: As a telemarketing representative, one of your most valuable assets may be knowledge of your company's products or services. Matching product or service benefits to a customer's needs begins with knowing what your company has to offer.

DEVELOP PRODUCT BENEFIT STATEMENTS

"My sons do the lawn work most of the time," says Mr. Osgoode. "Of course, I always check the oil before I start her up. I'm not sure the boys always remember."

"Our latest John Deere has a warning light that lights up when your oil is low. That would be helpful, wouldn't it?" you ask.

During a telephone call, a **potential** customer may reveal what product features he or she is looking for in a product. If you explain how the product will benefit this person, you may spark enough interest to make an appointment or a sale. Consider this:

Indicator	*Product Feature*	*Benefit Feature*
customer checks oil (sons may forget)	oil warning light for low oil level	"Our latest John Deere has a warning light that lights up when your oil is low. That would be helpful, wouldn't it?"

By carefully listening for indicators, and knowing what the product features are, you can develop a positive benefit statement and get the appointment to make that sale.

For this task you will develop benefit statements for different products. On page 161, you will find a customer indicator and product feature list. This list tells you the

- ▶ product or service you are selling
- ▶ customer indicators—what the customer likes or dislikes
- ▶ product features—strong points about your product or service

VISUALIZE THE WHOLE TASK

Before you start, think through the steps you will take to develop your product benefit statements. • What resources do you need? • How much time will it take you? • Do you need more information?

YOUR NOTES

Now, write down the steps you will follow. How will you develop product benefit statements?

First, I will find the list on page 161. Then, _____

_____

Use the customer indicator and product feature list on page 161 to develop product benefit statements. You may want to use the space below to write the benefit statements and copy your final statements on page 161.

A. _____

_____

B. _____

_____

C. _____

_____

TASK RECAP

▶ Did you end each statement with a phrase, like couldn't it, don't you, doesn't it?
▶ Did you include the product feature in the statement?

REVIEW YOUR PLAN

What did you do differently than you had planned? • What was difficult? • What was easy? • *Remember, as long as you linked the product benefit to the feature and indicator, you're on the right track.*

_____

_____

_____

Systems: Most telemarketing reps use computer systems to organize customer information. The more familiar they are with their information system, the more quickly they can assist customers.

ACCESS A COMPUTER FILE

In the story on page 36, you used a schedule to make an appointment for Mr. Osgoode, and you had Mr. Osgoode's address handy. How did you know all of this? You had a computer system that you used to organize and manage information.

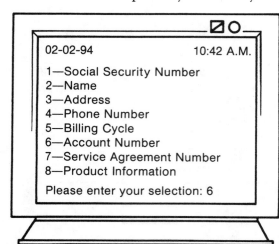

02-02-94	10:42 A.M.
1—Social Security Number	
2—Name	
3—Address	
4—Phone Number	
5—Billing Cycle	
6—Account Number	
7—Service Agreement Number	
8—Product Information	
Please enter your selection: 6	

Imagine your computer screen looks something like this: Your system only allows you to **access**, or open, a computer file from the **menu**. The menu is a directory of topics on a computer screen.

Say a customer calls with a problem. You answer, "C H & E Customer Service, may I have your account number please?"

The customer responds, "2234-96."

"Thank you, Ms. Olfin. I have your account information in front of me. How may I help you today?"

Here's how you used the system: You asked for the customer's account number, then typed "6" to access file number 6, *Account Number.* You typed in your caller's account number "2234-96." Your computer automatically brought up the customer's name and account information.

For this task you will decide which file to access in order to help a customer. You will use the customer calls list on page 43 for this task.

> ### VISUALIZE THE WHOLE TASK

Before you begin, think through the steps you will take to decide which file to access.
• What will you do first? • Do you need more information? • How much time will it take you? • Do you need other resources to make your decisions?

```
┌─────────────────────────────────────────────────────────────┐
│                         YOUR NOTES                          │
│                                                             │
│   How will you decide which file to access? What information might be helpful? │
│                                                             │
│   I will read through the customer calls first, then,_____ │
│                                                             │
│   _____  │
│                                                             │
└─────────────────────────────────────────────────────────────┘
```

COMPLETE THE TASK

Use the list below and the option menu on page 42 to decide which menu file to access. Fill in the blank with the appropriate option menu number (1–8).

OPTION NUMBER   **CUSTOMER CALLS**

_____ 1. "I haven't received my most recent bill. Can you check if it has been sent out?"

_____ 2. "I don't have my account number with me, but my telephone number is 555-1134."

_____ 3. "I'm having trouble using my new copier. Could you tell me how to change the ink?"

_____ 4. "I'm sorry, I'd rather not give you my social security number. Will my account number work?"

_____ 5. "I received some information about renewing my service plan. When does my original agreement end?"

_____ 6. "My name is Thompson, t-h-o-m-p-s-o-n, Jennifer A. Thompson."

TASK RECAP

▶ Did you check to make sure the option menu number corresponded to the file you wanted to access?

REVIEW YOUR PLAN

What steps did you follow? • How long did it actually take? • What resources did you actually use?

_____

_____

Interpersonal: Negotiating to arrive at a decision is an important part of a telemarketing representative's job.

MAKE A SALES CALL

"**Negotiating** is a cooperative and human process. . . . You achieve agreement, not victory." Gerard I. Nierenberg, *The Art of Negotiating*

For this task you will actually practice making a sales call and negotiating with a potential customer. You'll be negotiating to agree on a convenient appointment time. After you practice making the sales call, you will identify two key moments during the sales call. Your potential customer can be a classmate, teacher, friend, or family member.

At the beginning of this lesson, you read part of a sales call you made as a telemarketing rep for Power Mowers Unlimited.

One key moment of the sales call is at the very beginning. A positive sales call begins when you use the customer's name immediately. It's also important to introduce yourself and your company.

"Mr. Osgoode, this is _____ with Power Mowers Unlimited."

Other key moments during a successful sales call may be when you:

▶ state the purpose of your call
▶ ask survey-type questions to decide if the customer needs your product or service
▶ are honest
▶ ask what the customer likes about his or her current product—"What do you like most about your current riding mower?"
▶ introduce the benefits of your product
▶ provide two appointment options
▶ negotiate an appointment time and day

VISUALIZE THE WHOLE TASK

Think through the steps you will take to practice the sales call. • Who can help you? • How can you be prepared? • What will you do first? • How long do you think it will take? • Do you need more information?

```
┌─────────────────────────────────────────────────────────────┐
│                        YOUR NOTES                           │
├─────────────────────────────────────────────────────────────┤
│  How will you arrange the sales call? Who will be your       │
│  customer? How will you identify key sales moments?          │
│                                                              │
│  _____         │
│                                                              │
│  _____         │
│                                                              │
│  _____         │
│                                                              │
└─────────────────────────────────────────────────────────────┘
```

COMPLETE THE TASK

Use the telemarketing role-play script on page 163 to practice a sales call. A friend or a family member should play the part of Mr. Osgoode.

Once you have completed the script, identify two key moments during the sales call.

1. _____

2. _____

Which moments on the list on page 44 describe your two choices above? For example, did you state the purpose of your call or introduce yourself and your company?

1. _____

2. _____

TASK RECAP

- ▶ Did you use a warm and friendly tone?
- ▶ Did you identify two key points of the role play?
- ▶ What description fits each key moment?

REVIEW YOUR PLAN

How did you do? • Ask your customer how he or she felt. • Did your customer feel defensive when you asked the questions? • Comforted when you continued using his or her name?

_____

_____

Technology and Tools: Telemarketing reps use various tools and technology to complete their daily tasks. One of the tools may be a computer.

LEARN ABOUT A COMPUTER SOFTWARE SYSTEM

For this task you will ask a telemarketing representative to access (choose) one menu option and to explain when he or she might use that particular option. You will need to get permission to observe a telemarketing rep responding to a customer-service-type call.

Call a manufacturer or a telephone company in your area to find out if it has a telemarketing department. Explain that you would like to observe a telemarketer or a customer service rep answering a call. You will want to prepare what you are going to say before you call.

Next, complete this lesson, making any additional notes about your experience. You might want to make notes about:

▶ where you observed the rep
▶ what the office environment was like
▶ what education the rep had to use the computer
▶ how the rep knows which **menu option**, or **computer screen**, to access
▶ whether the rep uses a computer procedures manual

VISUALIZE THE WHOLE TASK

Before you start, think through the steps you will take to set up and complete your observations. • What will you do first? • Who will you call? • How much time do you think it will take? • What other people are involved?

YOUR NOTES

How will you set up your appointment? What steps will you follow to complete the task?

First, I will list friends and family who are or know customer service or telemarketing reps.

Then, I will call these two companies in my area that may have a telemarketing department:

_____

_____

Prepare a script of questions you want to ask the person you'll be observing. Using your script, go to the company you called and observe the telemarketing or customer service representative.

1. List the menu option you chose to have explained: _____

2. Write the reason the representative uses this option. (When? Why? How does it work?)

_____

_____

_____

_____

_____

_____

_____

TASK RECAP

▶ Did you answer all of the questions you had prepared?
▶ Were you able to identify the tools and technology the customer service or telemarketing rep used?
▶ Did you list and write a description of the option you chose?

Now that you've completed your observations and written an explanation of one option, what steps did you actually follow? • What additional information did you learn?

_____

_____

_____

_____

_____

USE WHAT YOU'VE LEARNED

You've been learning a variety of skills within the context of being a telemarketing representative. Some of these skills are

- ▶ organizing information
- ▶ allocating time for specific tasks
- ▶ using your judgment
- ▶ identifying key information

1. Name two other jobs that might require these skills. How might these skills be put to use?

   Example: a *teacher allocates time for a lesson*

   _____

   _____

   _____

2. Is there anywhere else you've used these skills? Where?

   Example: *at home, I use judgment when I decide which purchases are needs and which are wants*

   _____

   _____

   _____

3. Now that you have completed the tasks in this lesson, can you think of two new tasks at work or at home that you might try? What are they?

   _____

   _____

   _____

■■■ FINANCIAL SERVICES

The growth rate for jobs in the financial services industry is expected to be about the same as that for all jobs over the next 10 years. Workers in the financial services field do high-level clerical work that requires special skills and knowledge. They help companies and other organizations keep track of accounts and business **transactions.** These workers collect, organize, compute, and record numerical information.

SOME SKILLS YOU WILL PRACTICE IN THIS LESSON

▶ Understand a System
▶ Allocate Time
▶ Analyze and Interpret Information
▶ Serve Clients
▶ Select Technology

Public accountants provide their services to the public for a fee. Accountants who help you with your tax return are usually public accountants. They also audit, or go over, a company's or person's financial records to make sure the information is accurate. They also give advice about tax returns and suggestions about improving the way a company or person does business.

Private accountants are usually employed by a single business. They may analyze data and create financial statements and reports to suggest how a company might make better business decisions, including decisions about budgets and future purchases.

Government accountants provide many of the same services public and private accountants might provide. They are primarily responsible for controlling costs and compiling data about how government units do business.

All accountants perform their jobs based on basic financial practices and established procedures.

SOME RELATED JOBS

financial analyst
financial planner
stockbroker
economist

Tax Time

The challenge of tax time takes its toll on every employee at Dunn's Public Accounting Service, Inc. January through May, every year, is tax season, and it's the busiest time of year.

Every accountant has several daily appointments. **Data processors** are busy at computer terminals, the receptionist has lines holding, and more calls are coming in every minute.

You are a certified public accountant (CPA) who works long hours during tax season. In your first year with Dunn's, you are as prepared as you can be for your first year of tax preparation.

"It'll get easier," says Carolyn, another CPA. "It really helps to have Brian inputting the data into the computer. Two years ago, we did it all. With this new system, I've been preparing about three more returns a week."

"I think I'm starting to **understand the system** a little better. Brian just called and said he has the return review for ABC Title & Abstract printed and ready

for me. And I just got another call and have to **work another first appointment into this afternoon and find time to calculate my hours for each client**."

Carolyn laughs, "You wouldn't want to do mine, would you? I'm sure you have all the billing codes memorized by now. You do owe me for buying pizza last night."

"Did you forget about the Chinese food I bought the night before?" You smile, and obviously changing thoughts mention, "Adrienne called me last night and said, 'Daddy, are you going to be home in time to tell me a good-night story?' I made it just in time."

"It's tough, but just keep telling yourself it will even out after tax season," assures Carolyn.

"Well," you say, "I'd better get moving. I had a new client in yesterday. I need to **run through some questions with him this morning**. He's bringing in his receipts and other information this morning so I can **calculate depreciation on his rental property**."

"Don't forget, you told me to remind you to **print those spreadsheets**. I think we're both going to keep busy. What do you think?" asks Carolyn.

Without hesitating, you say, "Oh, yeah. You'd better keep that pizza delivery number handy. It looks like it'll be another late one."

An accountant works on many projects at the same time. Some information and forms must be obtained and completed before others. Think of this lesson as five tasks you might perform as an accountant.

SUMMARIZE THE TASKS

There are five tasks (highlighted in the story on page 50), that you will complete in this lesson. Some tasks have already been listed below for you. Skim the story to find all the tasks and write the two remaining tasks below in the appropriate category.

CATEGORY	TASK	ORDER	PAGE
Resources	*allocate time for appointments*	____	52
Information	_____	____	55
Systems	_____	____	58
Interpersonal	*review information with a client*	____	61
Technology and Tools	*use a computer to print a spreadsheet*	____	64

PLAN YOUR TIME

Think of this lesson as five tasks done by an accountant on a given day. You may need to do certain tasks before you can do others. In the ORDER column above, number the tasks 1 through 5 in the order you would complete them.

You may have chosen *allocate time for appointments* or another task as the first activity.

The page order of the tasks in this workbook is not necessarily the order in which you would do them. Follow the order that you decided above when you begin to work through the lesson.

THINK IT THROUGH

What will you need to do the tasks? • What other resources? • What other information? • Are other people involved?

Go to the task *you* listed as 1 and continue the lesson.

Resources: Allocating time to meet with clients and completing their financial records is especially important to accountants because they usually work on a deadline.

ALLOCATE TIME FOR CLIENTS

This is what your day as an accountant might look like on paper.

HOURS	FOR	SUBJECT	DESCRIPTION OF SERVICES	BILLING CODE	TIME HRS 1/10
8		8:30ᴬ			
	ABC Title, Inc.	– Income taxes	[Income tax - Business		
	Adam Calvin in office	– Review Organizer	Prep]		
9		– List of documents needed			
10	Mahoney + Hineman	10:35ᴬ – [Tax consult/projection]			
11	└ Betty Mahoney in office				
12	Lunch				
	Print spreadsheets – ABC Title, Inc. [N/c office time]	12:35ᴾ			
1	Desirable Delectables	1:30ᴾ [Reviewed '92 financial statements]			
2	└ Cassandra Bertulucci in office	2ᴾ – [Begin income tax prep] (business)			
3	ABC Title	– [Income tax prep business]			
4	Marco di Francesca in office	– [Income tax prep - Personal/ Individual]			
5	Li Ping	[Income tax prep - Personal/ Individual]			

DIARY AND WORK RECORD   11th Week · 78th Day · MARCH, 1993   **FRIDAY** MARCH, 1993 **19**

At the end of the day you have to calculate your **billable client hours**, which includes both actual appointments and the time you are working exclusively on that client's account. This includes assigning a billing code to the client time and totaling the hours and minutes to the nearest 1/10 (0.1). Once you have calculated the time and assigned billing codes to each time period, you forward a copy of your work record for computer input.

Look at the example below. It shows your appointment with Adam Calvin of ABC Title Company.

HOURS	FOR	SUBJECT	DESCRIPTION OF SERVICES		BILLING CODE	TIME HRS 1/10
8	[ABC Title, Inc.] Adam Calvin in office	8:30ᴬ − Income taxes − Review Organizer	[Income tax − Business prep]		51	2.00
9		− List of documents needed				

DIARY AND WORK RECORD — 11th Week • 78th Day • FRIDAY MARCH, 1993 **19**

Billing Category • Billing Code • Billable time

For this task you will calculate your billable client time for the day using the billing code listing on page 54.

VISUALIZE THE WHOLE TASK

Before you calculate your billable client time for the day, think through the steps you will take. • What will you do first? • Next? • What resources do you need? • Do you need more information?

YOUR NOTES
How will you go about calculating your billable client hours? Write down the steps you will follow.
First, I will locate the billing code listing. Then, I will _____
_____
_____

Use the billing code listing below and the work record on page 52 to calculate your billable client time and assign billing codes to the time.

Category/Billing Code Listing

No	Category Description	Billable ?	Available ?	No	Code Description	Time Or Expense	Billing Rate	Taxable ?
1	WRITE-UP SERVICES	Y	Y	10	FINANCIAL STATEMENTS	T	1	
				11	PAYROLL TAX RETURNS	T	1	
				12	PAYROLL PREPARATION	T	1	
				15	PERSONAL PROPERTY TAX	T	1	
2	COMPILATION SERVICES	Y	Y	20	COMPILED FINANCIAL STATEMENTS	T	2	
3	REVIEW SERVICES	Y	Y	30	REVIEWED FINANCIAL STATEMENTS	T	2	
4	AUDIT SERVICES	Y	Y	40	AUDITED FINANCIAL STATEMENTS	T	2	
5	INCOME TAX SERVICES	Y	Y	50	INDIVIDUAL INCOME TAX	T	3	
				51	BUSINESS INCOME TAX	T	3	
				52	TAX CONSULTATION & PROJECTION	T	3	
				55	TAX EXAMINATION	T	3	
				252	TAX CONSULTATION & PROJECTION LEVEL II	T	5	
				255	TAX EXAM LEVEL II	T	5	
8	NONCHARGEABLE TIME	N	Y	80	NONCHARGEABLE OFFICE	T	0	
				81	FIRM ADMINISTRATION	T	0	
				82	CONTINUING EDUCATION	T	0	

Cross Reference

Billing Rate
1 = $50/HR.
2 = $65/HR.
3 = $75/HR.
4 = $100/HR.
5 = $125/HR.

TASK RECAP

► Did you match the billing category to the categories on the listing?

► Did you express the time to the nearest 1/10 (.01)?

► Did you double-check your calculations and the billing code you assigned?

Now that you've calculated your billable client time and assigned a billing code, what steps did you actually follow? • How much time did it actually take?

_____

_____

Information: Accountants analyze, interpret, and organize information and data to keep records and make financial recommendations to companies and individuals. Information may come in the form of tables, graphs, lists, journals, or charts.

CALCULATE DEPRECIATION

One of the tasks an accountant may perform when preparing a client's tax return is calculating **depreciation**.

An apartment rental building and the equipment purchased for business use will eventually wear out and not be useful anymore to the owner. This usefulness is recorded as depreciation. Look at the bottom part of Marco di Francesca's rent and royalty income and expenses sheet on page 165. It shows the dates he bought three pieces of equipment for an apartment building he owns and the cost of each item.

For this task you will calculate depreciation on his equipment, using a master tax guide depreciation table, a depreciation worksheet on page 56, and the tax organizer on page 165.

Study the sample depreciation calculation for the refrigerator on the following page.

Step 1 Determine the depreciation rate using the master tax guide table.

According to tax laws, the cost of a refrigerator can be depreciated over a seven-year recovery period. Because this is the first year Marco purchased and is using the equipment, you will calculate depreciation for the first recovery year, using the master tax guide depreciation Table 3. Follow the row across to the seven-year column.

Master Tax Guide Depreciation Table

Table 3. General Depreciation System
        Applicable Depreciation Method: 200 or 150 Percent
        Declining Balance Switching to Straight Line
        Applicable Recovery Periods: 3, 5, 7, 10, 15, 20 years
        Applicable Convention: Mid-quarter (property placed in service in second quarter)

If the Recovery Year is:	3-year	5-year	7-year	10-year	15-year	20-year
			the Depreciation Rate is:			
1	41.67	25.00	17.85	12.50	6.25	4.688
2	38.89	30.00	23.47	17.50	9.38	7.148
3	14.14	18.00	16.76	14.00	8.44	6.612
4	5.30	11.37	11.97	11.20	7.59	6.116
5		11.37	8.87	8.96	6.83	5.658
6		4.26	8.87	7.17	6.15	5.233
7			8.87	6.55	5.91	4.841
8			3.33	6.55	5.90	4.478
9				6.56	5.91	4.463
10				6.55	5.90	4.463
11				2.46	5.91	4.463
12					5.90	4.463
13					5.91	4.463
14					5.90	4.463
15					5.91	4.462
16					2.21	4.463
17						4.462
18						4.463
19						4.462
20						4.463
21						1.673

first year → (pointing to Recovery Year 1)

Step 2 Calculate depreciation expense on the worksheet below by using the formula:

Purchase Price	×	**Depreciation**	=	**Depreciation Expense**
(in Tax Organizer)		(in Tax Guide)		
$600.00	×	17.85%	=	$107.10

You may use your calculator to compute

(6)(0)(0)(×)(1)(7)(·)(8)(5)(%)(=)(107.10)

DEPRECIATION WORKSHEET
PROPERTY A

NAME *Marco A. di Francesca*

Your social security number 505 : 55 : 1234

DESCRIPTION OF PROPERTY	COST OR OTHER BASIS	DATE ACQUIRED	RATE (%) OR LIFE	MACRS METHOD	DEPRECIATION FOR THIS YEAR 19 93
Refrigerator	$600.00	5/6/93	17.85%		$107.10
Air conditioning unit					
Furnace					
				Total	$

Step 3 Enter the total depreciation expense on Schedule E, Line 20. (*Hint:* Write the three individual depreciation figures and then the total.)

20 Depreciation expense or depletion (see page E–2)	20				20

To review, this task involves three steps:

1. Calculate the year-one depreciation expense on the air conditioning unit (10 years) and the furnace (7 years).

2. Calculate the total amount for all three depreciated items.

3. Enter the total amount of depreciation expenses on the Schedule E tax return form on page 169.

VISUALIZE THE WHOLE TASK

Before you calculate Marco di Francesca's total depreciation, read back through the steps above. • Think through the steps you will take to calculate each item's depreciation and how you will complete the task. • What will you do first?

COMPLETE THE TASK

Use the master tax guide depreciation table on pages 55 or 167 and the depreciation worksheet below (and your notes) to calculate Marco di Francesca's total depreciation expense. Then enter that amount on the supplemental income and loss sheet (Schedule E) on page 169.

DEPRECIATION WORKSHEET
PROPERTY A

NAME

Your social security number

DESCRIPTION OF PROPERTY	COST OR OTHER BASIS	DATE ACQUIRED	RATE (%) OR LIFE	MACRS METHOD	DEPRECIATION FOR THIS YEAR 19

TASK RECAP

▶ Did you use Table 3 to find the rates for 7 years and 10 years?
▶ Did you double-check your calculations?

REVIEW YOUR PLAN

Now that you've calculated the depreciation expense and entered the amount on Schedule E, what steps did you actually follow? • What resources did you use?

Systems: In an accounting office, an accountant plays an important role in the work flow process. Usually, a standard process is established by the company to ensure quality and efficiency when providing services to customers.

UNDERSTAND THE WORK FLOW SYSTEM

As part of your tax season training, your supervisor has sent you the following memo:

To:	New Staff Accountants
From:	Winthrop Cooke, Managing Partner *WC*
Subject:	Tax Preparation
Date:	December 10, 1993

As we approach a new tax season, I am happy to inform you that you will no longer be responsible for the bulk of the **tax return** computer input. We have hired a data processor, Brian Lowenstein, for the season.

Review the attached work flow and respond in writing to me by December 15 with questions or comments about the process. I am open, as always, for recommendations, clarifications, questions, etc.

We will review and discuss all issues at next Monday's staff meeting on December 16th.

Study the work flowchart from Dunn's Public Accounting Service, Inc. on page 171. (Part of the flowchart is shown below.) You will see that accountants may work independently and with other office staff. According to the work flow, a procedure has been established to work with tax preparation clients.

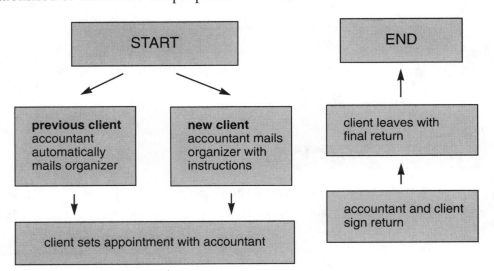

Previous clients who may have had Dunn's Public Accounting Service prepare their taxes the past year will automatically be mailed a **tax organizer** (see page 173). New clients who request Dunn's services for the first time will be mailed a letter of instructions with a tax organizer.

According to the chart, you, the accountant, mail the tax organizer to the client and include instructions. Because the managing partner has asked for recommendations, you might suggest the following two ideas after you list your responsibilities.

1. For previous clients, the administrative assistant accesses the previous clients' files; the accountant reviews the list for accuracy; the administrative assistant prepares and mails the instructions letter and organizer to previous clients.

2. For new clients, the accountant accepts the new client and forwards the name to be added to the mailing list; the administrative assistant prepares the instructions letter and organizer; the accountant signs the letter and forwards it to the new client.

You may choose to make more than one suggestion or ask more than one question in your written response to the managing partner. *You may want to follow the same memo format on the previous page. Don't forget to initial the memo by your name.*

For this task you will need to prepare a written response to the managing partner, Winthrop Cooke.

VISUALIZE THE WHOLE TASK

Before you begin your response, read through the information above. • Think through the steps you will follow to understand the system and write a response to the managing partner. • How much time will it take you? • What resources might be helpful? • A dictionary?

YOUR NOTES
How will you prepare a written response to the managing partner? Write down what steps you will take.
First, I will read through the work flowchart. Then, I will _____
_____
_____
_____

On a separate sheet of paper, print neatly or type your written response to your supervisor, Winthrop Cooke. Use the space below to make notes and organize your thoughts.

QUESTIONS OR CLARIFICATIONS

_____

_____

_____

_____

RECOMMENDATIONS OR SUGGESTIONS

_____

_____

_____

_____

TASK RECAP

► Did you write clear, complete sentences?
► Is your written response spelled correctly?
► Did you print neatly or type your response?

REVIEW YOUR PLAN

Now that you've written your response to Winthrop Cooke, what steps did you actually follow? • What resources, other information, or technology did you use?

_____

_____

_____

Interpersonal: Serving a client's needs is an important part of the role of an accountant. Confidentiality is a key requirement in an advisor/client relationship.

"No matter what is discussed in our meeting, the information you provide and the questions you answer are in the strictest confidence between you and me. I may need to share the information with other professionals within my company, like my supervisor, but it would be only in your best interest. If anyone other than you calls me to ask if you are receiving services, or about your account, I will simply say, 'That information is confidential.' "

INTERVIEW A CLIENT

In many occupations, interviewing is a way to gather information about someone's situation or a problem that needs to be solved. In this case, Will and Carolyn meet with clients to discuss their financial situations and to gather information that will help them prepare their tax returns efficiently and accurately.

Dealing with clients may be difficult if they don't understand the purpose for your asking a question.

A complete tax organizer (shown on page 173) is a way for a client to begin organizing all the information and data necessary to prepare a tax return. The client is responsible for completing as much of the organizer as possible before the initial appointment.

In some cases, clients do not complete the tax organizer before they arrive for their appointments. You review the information with them, filling in any empty blanks. For example, if the person has left the *Age* column blank, you might ask, "What was your age, as of December 31?" to complete the top part of the form shown below.

Personal Information, Dependents and Wages ___ 3

Personal Information

| | Y – Yes | N– No |

	First Name and Initial	Last Name	Social Security Number	Presidential Election Contribution
Taxpayer			: :	—
Spouse			: :	—

	Occupation	Age on 12 / 31	X if Blind	Date Deceased Mo Da Yr	X if Dependent of Another
Taxpayer		___	—	: :	—
Spouse		___	—	: :	—

To complete the *Code* column under the Dependents section, you will find a code descriptor box on the part of the tax organizer shown below.

|||| Federal tax regulations require children 1 year of age or older to have a social security number.

C – Dependent child living with taxpayer		XN – Dependent child not living with taxpayer and release	
O – Other dependents		of claim to exemption should be filed	
N – Dependent child not living with taxpayer		E – Child qualifying you for earned income credit	
		(household member, not a dependent)	

Did dependent have over $2300 income? ⌐

TSJ	State	First Name, Initial and Last Name	Social Security Number	Age	Relationship	Months Lived in Your Home	X if Disabled	Y / N	Code
—	—		: :	—		—	—	—	
—	—		: :	—		—	—	—	
—	—		: :	—		—	—	—	
—	—		: :	—		—	—	—	
—	—		: :	—		—	—	—	

In this example, the client claims her daughter as a dependent, but the child lives with her grandmother. You would put an *N* in the *Code* column.

When completing the Wages and Salaries section, the client will need to have a W-2 form. If the W-2 form is not available, the client may refer to the sample W-2 form at the back of the book on page 167.

For this task you will role-play a client interview with an adult using the personal information sheet on page 17⁹ of the tax organizer and fill in all the appropriate blanks.

VISUALIZE THE WHOLE TASK

Before you begin your client interview (with a classmate, family member, or friend), think through the steps you will take to set up the interview and complete the personal information sheet. • What will you do first? •What resources do you need? • What other information will be useful?

YOUR NOTES
How will you set up the interview? Who will be your client? Write the steps you will take.
First, I will review the personal information sheet. Then, I will ask an adult to role-play the
client. Next, I will

COMPLETE THE TASK

Use the personal information, dependents and wages sheet on page 173 to role-play a client interview. Complete the form, filling in all the appropriate blanks. Remember, your client may use his or her own information or the wage information provided on the sample W-2 form on page 167.

Use the space below to prepare questions you might ask to gather the information.

TASK RECAP

► Did you ask the questions you prepared?
► Did you ask for the spellings of uncommon names?
► Did you use the appropriate code for the dependents?

REVIEW YOUR PLAN

Now that you've completed the interview and personal information sheet, what steps did you actually follow? • Who helped you?

Technology and Tools: Accountants may use computers, calculators, and custom-designed computer software to prepare financial statements and tax returns. Spreadsheet software programs are computerized column pads that are used by many accountants.

LEARN ABOUT SPREADSHEET TECHNOLOGY

For this task you will ask an accountant to access (choose) a spreadsheet and explain how and why he or she uses a computerized spreadsheet. You will need to get permission to observe an accountant on the job.

Call an accounting firm, private company, or government agency in your area to find out if it has an accountant. Explain that you would like to observe an accountant working on a computerized spreadsheet. You will want to prepare what you are going to say before you call.

Next, complete this lesson, making any additional notes about your experience. You might want to make notes about

▶ what other financial **software** programs they use
▶ how they use those programs
▶ what education the accountant had in using the computer

VISUALIZE THE WHOLE TASK

Before you start making calls to set up an appointment, think through the steps you will take to complete your observations. • Who will you call? • What other information do you need?

YOUR NOTES
Write down the steps you will take to complete the task. Be specific about how you will arrange transportation and what questions you plan to ask. _____ _____ _____ _____ _____

Prepare a script of questions you want to ask the accountant you'll be observing. Using your script, go to the company where you set up your appointment and observe the accountant. Ask the accountant if you may have a spreadsheet to bring back to class.

1. List the computer spreadsheet software the accountant uses.

   _____

2. Write how the accountant uses the spreadsheet. (How does it work? When is it used? Why is it used?)

   _____

   _____

   _____

   _____

   _____

3. On a separate sheet of paper, write three or more paragraphs explaining why you agree or disagree that there is an advantage in using a computerized spreadsheet.

TASK RECAP

► Were all your questions you had prepared answered?
► Were you able to identify how a computer spreadsheet helps accountants in their daily tasks?

Now that you've completed your observation and learned about spreadsheets, what steps did you actually follow? • How long did you observe the accountant?

   _____

   _____

   _____

   _____

USE WHAT YOU'VE LEARNED

You've been learning a variety of skills within the context of an accountant. Some of these skills are

- ▶ analyzing information
- ▶ scanning for details
- ▶ keeping client confidence
- ▶ filling out forms

1. Name two other jobs that might require these skills. How might these skills be put to use?

   Example: a ***psychologist*** *analyzes patient information to make a diagnosis*

   _____

   _____

   _____

2. Is there anywhere else you've used these skills? Where?

   _____

   _____

   _____

3. Now that you have completed the tasks in this lesson, can you think of two new tasks at work or at home that you might try? What are they?

   _____

   _____

   _____

   _____

■■■ HOSPITALITY SERVICES

The hospitality services industry is expected to grow at a faster rate than the average growth rate for all industries over the next decade. Many of these jobs will be entry level as other workers move into more highly skilled positions. Workers in this industry perform tasks such as cleaning, food preparation, operating simple machines, and personal services.

SOME SKILLS YOU WILL PRACTICE IN THIS LESSON

- ▶ Allocate Human Resources
- ▶ Communicate Information
- ▶ Understand a System
- ▶ Serve a Customer
- ▶ Select Technology

A food service manager is primarily responsible for all phases of a food service operation. Food service managers may work in hospitals, fine dining restaurants, hotels, nursing homes, or schools, for example. Depending on the size of the organization, the food service manager may supervise other assistant managers and oversee the whole operation, or may directly supervise kitchen and dining room staff.

Food service managers may work with budgets, schedule staff requirements for events, or order food or supplies needed. By understanding the responsibilities of the food service staff (assistant managers, cooks, servers, and busers), the food service manager ensures that the organization delivers quality service to its customers.

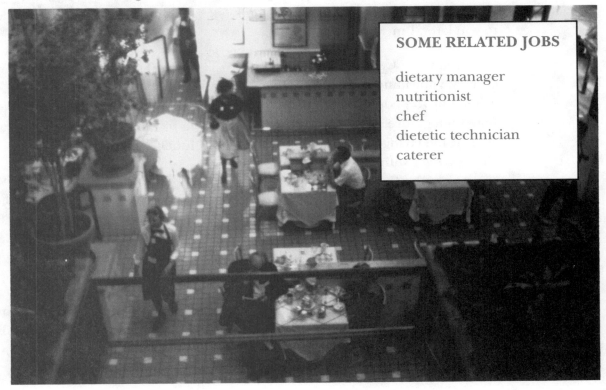

SOME RELATED JOBS

dietary manager
nutritionist
chef
dietetic technician
caterer

Hotel Hospitality

When you were in training, they never told you it might be like today. It's Wednesday, July 7.

The minute you walk into your office at 8:00 A.M., the telephone rings. There's a stack of pink message forms in your box waiting to be answered and twice the paperwork as you had yesterday.

As you answer the telephone, a server peeks into your office and whispers, "The dishwasher is broken again."

You close your eyes and try to focus on your telephone conversation with Celeste Reed, the sales and catering manager of the hotel. Celeste is always brief with her calls. "The good news is I thought we were going to have five changes for this Friday's Ladies' League luncheon. Now we only have two changes. The bad news is that we need to figure on 90 instead of 75 people. I'm faxing the updated event worksheet to you. I thought you'd like to know the changes were coming. I'll talk to you later, I'm sure."

After thanking Celeste for calling so quickly, your mind starts racing. Ninety instead of 75 people. That means **scheduling more staff, informing the chef of the changes, and talking the changes over with Mrs. Lavinier.** You remember the flooded restroom.

As you stand up, James peeks his head in and says he's fixed the dishwasher. James is a great server. He's helped you out more times than you can count—coming in on his day off, helping out a fellow server with a slow table, to name just a few.

After only 15 minutes at work, you realize today will be full with the changes on the

Ladies' League luncheon and overseeing today's events.

There are two small events in the banquet rooms today. One has a sit-down lunch for 50 people. James and three other servers are scheduled to work.

The other event at 4:30 P.M. requires only two servers for soft drinks, coffee, and tea, and tables set up at the entrance of the banquet room.

At 8:30 A.M., you sit down to work on the Ladies' League luncheon. You have half an hour before the servers start coming in to work on the Ladies' League luncheon changes.

At 9:30 A.M., one of the busers scheduled for the sit-down lunch is half an hour late. You **use the staff sheet** to find out who is available for work today and begin making calls to get someone to cover for the missing buser.

You also want to **find out about the new industrial dishwashers available** because you'd like to put in a purchase order to buy a new one.

A food service manager's responsibility is to maintain efficient, quality service at all times. Maintaining control and organization when problems arise promotes staff and customer satisfaction. Each task you will perform in this lesson is an example of what you may do as a food service manager.

SUMMARIZE THE TASKS

The five tasks you will accomplish in this lesson were mentioned in the story on page 68. Before you look at the story, try to remember two of the tasks. Now list after the appropriate category the five tasks you will complete.

CATEGORY	TASK	ORDER	PAGE
Resources	_____	____	70
Information	_____	____	72
Systems	_____	____	75
Interpersonal	_____	____	78
Technology and Tools	_____	____	80

(*Hint:* Scheduling staff is a human resources task, and, in this case, the staff sheet is a system used to organize staff members' hours.)

PLAN YOUR TIME

Think of this lesson as tasks done by a food service manager on a given workday. You may need to do certain tasks before you can do others. In the ORDER column above, number the tasks in the order you would complete them. You may have chosen *talk the changes over with Mrs. Lavinier* as the first activity.

The page order of the tasks in this workbook is not necessarily the order in which you would do them. Follow the order that you decided above when you begin to work through the lesson.

THINK IT THROUGH

What will you need to do the tasks? • What resources? • What other information? • Are other people involved?

Go to the task *you* listed above as 1 and continue the lesson.

Resources: In the hospitality services industry, scheduling enough, but not too many staff to cover the work load is possibly one of the most difficult tasks for a manager. Managers look at experience and use guidelines to schedule the staff necessary for a given shift. When the work load changes, so do the staff requirements. Adjusting schedules to meet the needs of your customers helps you provide quality service.

SCHEDULE SERVING STAFF

Mrs. Lavinier has told you about the Ladies' League luncheon changes a few days before the event will actually happen. Hopefully, you will have enough time to schedule more staff to cover the luncheon. You have prepared the following schedule for the Ladies' League luncheon based on:

Guidelines for Ladies' League luncheon
total number of guests (75 + 10 = 85)
budget requirements of customer ($12– $15 per person)
type of event (sit-down lunch)

You will be using a cook, food preparers, and servers for the luncheon. (A complete listing of staff is found on pages 175 and 177.)

Staff Schedule	Ladies' League luncheon
	Shift
J. Goodman	8 A.m. – 4 p.m.
G. Graham	8 A.m. – 4 p.m.
K. Rene	8 A.m. – 4 p.m.
C. Lai	10 A.m. – 4 A.m.
M. Brown	10 A.M. – 6 p.m.
S. Chung	10 A.M. – 6 P.M.
M. Farro	10 A.M. – 6 P.M.
R. Ferraro	10 A.M. – 6 P.M.
D. Lawson	10 A.M. – 6 P.M.

Originally, you had scheduled one server for two tables, having one server cover the extra guests remaining. You will use the same guideline in this task. (75 guests + 10 extra = 85 guests; 8 seats per table = 10 tables, plus 1 table with 5 guests)

Because you always prepare enough food and space for an additional 10 guests and Mrs. Lavinier has requested service for 90, you will need to revise the staff schedule.

For this task you will recalculate the table requirements *(Mrs. Lavinier told you about the changes in your conversation on page 179.)* **You will also add one server and one food preparer to the staff schedule on page 185.**

(Mrs. Lavinier told you about the changes in your conversation on page 179.)

VISUALIZE THE WHOLE TASK

Before you begin recalculating and revising, think through all the steps this task involves. • What resources will you use? • Do you need more information?

YOUR NOTES
Write down the steps you will follow to revise the staff schedule. What will you do first? Second?
I will review the section entitled "Understand a Spreadsheet." Then, I will skim the event
worksheets on page 78 to see how the table setup has changed. Next, I will

COMPLETE THE TASK

Revise the staff schedule on page 70 for the Ladies' League luncheon, according to Mrs. Lavinier's requests. *Use the staff spreadsheets on pages 175 and 177 to add one server and one food preparer to the schedule on page 185. You will notice on the spreadsheets that some staff have not worked the number of hours they requested. Give those workers priority as you add staff for 7/9.*

TASK RECAP

▶ Did you find the staff schedule?
▶ Did you remember to recalculate the servers needed based on the table arrangements, having one server cover the extra head table?

REVIEW YOUR PLAN

What worked for you? • Did you need to review how to use a spreadsheet?

Information: A food service manager communicates in many ways. You may write on forms or documents, conduct a staff meeting, or discreetly make suggestions to help a staff member do a better job. Whether you are completing a formal document or writing an informal note, the information you communicate needs to be clear, specific, and concise.

WRITE AN INFORMATIONAL NOTE

Have you ever written or received a telephone message that you had a hard time understanding? You may have received a message that looks something like this:

> Dave,
>
> Call me ASAP about the ABC Town. on the 10th — need cx.
>
> K.

What's the purpose of a message or note? To communicate information or instructions in written form, right? Compare the note written above to the note shown below. Which note is more clear and complete?

> TO: Bob Hirsh, Maintenance Manager
>
> FROM: Mario Peoples, Food Service Manager
>
> DATE: July 3
>
> RE: Kiwanis meeting microphones
>
> On July 7, in the Portsmouth Room, Larry Batesman will go over the room setup with you at 9:30 A.M. He wants you to explain how to use the three hand-held microphones, step-by-step. I'll be there at 10 A.M.
>
> Thanks,
> *Mario*
> Mario

Notice the details in the second note. The note explains clearly *who, what, where, when, what time,* and *how,* eliminating the chance of miscommunicating.

For this task you will write a note to inform the chef of menu changes or clarifications for the Ladies' League luncheon this Friday based on the conversation you had with Mrs. Lavinier this morning. *(See page 179.)*

(See page 179.)

Before you start your note to Chef Jerome Goodman, look back over the detailed note on page 72. • Think through the steps you will take to write the note. • What will you do first? • How much time will it take you? • Do you need more information before you can write the note? • Where can you find the information you need? • What resources might be helpful? • *Remember, you can use any information found in this lesson.*

YOUR NOTES

How will you make sure your note to the chef about the Ladies' League luncheon is clear and detailed? What will you include? What will you do first?

First, I will find out what changes were made to the menu by reading the conversation with

Mrs. Lavinier. Then, _____

_____

_____

COMPLETE THE TASK

Use the "Things to do" note on the next page to write a note to the chef about the luncheon menu changes. You may want to use the extra space provided below to make notes before you copy your final note to the chef.

_____

_____

_____

Things to do...

_____

_____

_____

_____

_____

_____

_____

_____

_____

TASK RECAP

► Did you write whom the note was from?

► Were you specific about the menu changes?

► Did you avoid using any **abbreviations**?

► When you were unsure, did you check your spelling?

► Did you write clear details about which event, when, at what time?

REVIEW YOUR PLAN

Now that you've completed your note to the chef about the menu changes, what steps did you actually follow? • What resources and other information were helpful? • Where did you find the information?

_____

_____

_____

_____

Systems: Some computer systems print out reports, organize large amounts of information, and perform many math computations quickly. On some jobs, you use a computerized spreadsheet, a type of printed report, to organize data. Using a spreadsheet, you can make changes or additions to numbers and information, and the computer program will automatically calculate and organize your changes.

UNDERSTAND A SPREADSHEET

It's 9:30 P.M. and one of the busers scheduled for the sit-down lunch is one-half hour late. You *use the staff sheet* to begin making calls to get someone to cover for her.

One way a food service manager may organize staff information or shift schedules is by using information systems. On a spreadsheet, you can create a system to organize numbers and information much like a table or chart with rows and columns.

▶ A row reads *left to right*, labeled with numbers
▶ A column reads *top to bottom*, labeled with letters

Each square is commonly known as a *cell*. In the sample below, *Food Service Staff* is in *cell A1*.

In this lesson, the spreadsheet includes numbers (data) and characters (letters or words) that you can choose to be printed or left off the spreadsheet. Because the computer spreadsheet program can process information quickly, you can calculate and recalculate numbers within seconds. You can also sort (organize) numbers and information in many ways. Look at the sample section of a spreadsheet below.

Spreadsheet

	A	B	C	D	E	F	G	H	I	J	K
1	Food Service Staff	Telephone	Req.	Hours							Weekly Total
2	Assistant Managers			7/3	7/4	7/5	7/6	7/7	7/8	7/9	
3	Ching, Lei	731-4483	40+	0	0	8	8	9	8	8	41
4	Diaz, Domingo	299-6372	40+	10	10	9	8	9	0	0	46
5	Luggen, Kurt	941-1141	40+	8	0	8	9	0	8	8	41
6	Suravich, Catherine	297-0776	25+	0	10	0	0	0	8	9	27
7											
8											

You may ask, why would I organize staff members' names alphabetically? Think about it. What if you needed to contact a staff person about a time card by telephone. If 60 or more employees' names were listed randomly (in no certain order), how long would it take to find a specific telephone number?

Spreadsheet

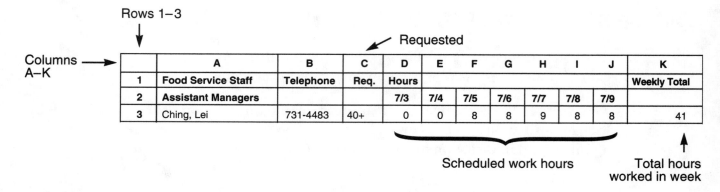

Find column A, row 3 (also called *cell A3*). You should find Lei Ching's name, who is an assistant manager (cell A2). Read across the row from left to right to find his telephone number, requested hours of work, daily hours, and weekly total.

For how many hours was Lei Ching scheduled to work on 7/9? How many hours did he work during the week?

If you say that he was scheduled to work for 8 hours on 7/9 and had a weekly total of 41, you're on the right track. You may want to use a ruler to help you follow across the row or down the column.

Compare cells C3 and K3. What does the information in these two columns tell you?

C3 tells you that Lei Ching has requested 40+ (40 or more) hours. K3 is Lei's weekly total of 41 hours.

For this task you will use the staff spreadsheets on pages 175 and 177 to find out which busers are available to be scheduled for this afternoon's luncheon.

VISUALIZE THE WHOLE TASK

Visualize what this task involves. • *Think about how the spreadsheet organizes information systematically, and how you can use the spreadsheet to find information.* • What other information do you need? • What other resources do you need to find and use? • How much time do you think it will take you?

YOUR NOTES

How will you find out what busers are available for this afternoon's luncheon? What will you do first?

First, I will locate the spreadsheets on pages 175 and 177. Then, I will find the Busers

section in column A on the Food Services Staff spreadsheet. Next, I will locate today's

column.

Melissa Smith is the missing buser. Use the space provided below to write the names and telephone numbers of the busers who might be able to come in for Melissa. Make a check (✔) by the buser who has **priority** over the others. *You won't need to add any more lines to the space below.*

Name   Telephone Number

_____   _____

_____   _____

_____   _____

_____   _____

TASK RECAP

▶ Did you follow the row *across* from each buser's name to the July 7 column?
▶ Did you compare columns C and K to decide who needed more hours?

Now that you've listed the busers who might be available, go back to your notes.
• Did you follow the steps you planned? • Did it take you longer or less time than you expected?

_____

_____

Interpersonal: The hospitality services industry is customer-oriented. Customers' plans or requests may change daily. Listening carefully and responding quickly to customers' needs can result in customer satisfaction and repeat business.

CHANGE PLANS TO MEET A CUSTOMER'S NEEDS

Have friends ever forgotten to tell you about a change in plans? Based on the information you were given, you expected a certain outcome. Unfortunately, you didn't have the correct information.

As you read in the story, Mrs. Lavinier changed some of the information about her luncheon plans. It is hotel policy that you contact Mrs. Lavinier by telephone to discuss any changes or additions to the original plans. Celeste Reed, the sales and catering manager, faxed you the two event worksheets shown below (in reduced form) that you use to plan menus, staff requirements, and room requirements.

Event Worksheet
Food Service

Company __Ladies' League__   Contact __Mrs. Margaret Lavinier__
Address __P.O. Box 351, Walnut Hills__   Phone/Fax __515-722-0232__
Event Date __July 9__   Time (begin/end) __12 PM – 2 PM__
Number of Guests __75__   Budget per person __$12–15__

Style:

- o   cake and punch   o   champagne
- o   hors d'oeuvres   o   wine
- o   buffet   o   cocktails
- X   sit-down   X   soft drinks
- o   _____   X   __hot coffee/hot tea__

The Menu:

__Main course: chicken kiev, broccoli, baked potato with choice of butter, sour cream, or both__
__Salad: iceberg lettuce with choice of ranch or peppercorn dressing__
__Dessert: baked apples with cinnamon__

Cost/person __$13__ x Total guests __75__ = Total Cost __$975__
Deposit Paid __$500__ on __June 24__
Client Signature __Margaret Lavinier__ Date __June 24__
Balance Due __$670__ on __July 5__
Sales/Catering Manager __Celeste Reed__ Date __June 24__

**Call sales/catering manager at 550-5550 with questions or problems

---

Event Worksheet
Maintenance and Setup

Company __Ladies' League__   Contact __Mrs. Margaret Lavinier__
Address __P.O. Box 351, Walnut Hills__ Phone/Fax __515-722-0232__
Room (Banquet Hall) __Van Meter__   Occupancy __120__
Date reserved __July 9__   from __9:30__ am/pm to __4__ am/pm

Equipment includes (specify type when appropriate):

- X   tables __Round (8 persons each)__
- X   chairs
- X   linens (tablecloth, table skirt, napkins) __white cloth, pink linen napkins__
- o   barware (liquor assortment, wine only, beer only) _____
- o   _____
- o   _____
- o   _____

Service includes:

- X   servers   o   bartenders   X   cleanup
- X   setup   o   security   o   _____

Total cost __$350__ Deposit paid __$350__ on __June 24__
Client signature __Margaret Lavinier__ Date __June 24__
Balance Due_____ on _____
Sales/Catering Mgr. __Celeste Reed__ Date __June 24__

**Call sales/catering manager at 550-5550 with questions or problems

---

For this task you will role-play the telephone conversation on pages 179 and 181, with a friend or family member (playing Mrs. Margaret Lavinier), and make changes on the event worksheets on page 78 for the Ladies' League luncheon.

Before you begin, visualize what steps you will take to arrange the role-play and how you will make changes on the event worksheets. • What information do you need? • What resources do you need? • How will you arrange the role-play? • Who will help you? • *Remember, you will need to make the changes or corrections while you are talking on the telephone. You may want to become familiar with the event worksheets before you begin the role-play.*

YOUR NOTES
Write down the steps you will take to arrange the role-play, and make changes on the event worksheets during the telephone conversation. *I will find the event worksheets on page 78 and read through them carefully. Then, I will*   *arrange for someone to role-play Mrs. Lavinier. Next, I will*

COMPLETE THE TASK

Use the telephone conversation role-play, making changes or corrections on the event worksheets on page 78 where appropriate. Write your initials and the date by the changes or corrections you made.

TASK RECAP

▶ Did you make the changes or corrections while you were talking with Mrs. Lavinier?

▶ Did you initial and date the changes?

REVIEW YOUR PLAN

Now that you've revised the Ladies' League luncheon event worksheets, what steps did you actually follow?

Technology and Tools: Food service management requires working with many different types of tools and technology. Dishwashers, food slicers, and ovens are just a few examples of technology. You may find that the larger and more complicated equipment gets, the more expensive it is.

LEARN ABOUT FOOD SERVICE EQUIPMENT

When something breaks down in a hotel or a restaurant, you will generally find that it gets fixed quickly. Of course, if a restaurant is known especially for its grilled chicken, and the grill doesn't work, how long do you think it will be in business?

For this task you will go to a cafeteria or a restaurant and talk to the food service manager about the equipment the cafeteria or restaurant has. You may choose to go to the cafeteria or restaurant in:

- ▶ a school
- ▶ a business complex
- ▶ a hotel
- ▶ a fine dining establishment
- ▶ a hospital

You will want to prepare what you are going to say before you call and set up the appointment to meet with the food service manager. Although you may learn about many types of equipment on your visit, choose one to write about.

To complete this task you will write a paragraph about one piece of equipment or one tool, explaining the uses and benefits of that particular model or style. Be sure to include the name, model, and style.

VISUALIZE THE WHOLE TASK

Before you start, think through the steps you will take to set up, complete, and record your food service visit. • How will you choose which piece of equipment or tool you are going to write about? • What other information do you need? • What resources do you need to gather?

YOUR NOTES
Write down the steps you will follow to arrange a cafeteria or a restaurant visit and how and what equipment you will choose to write about.
_____
_____

Arrange a visit and appointment with the food service manager at the cafeteria or restaurant of your choice. Use the space below to prepare questions before your visit. Write a paragraph on the uses and benefits of the equipment or tool you choose on another sheet of paper.

QUESTIONS

What equipment do you use? • What tools do you use? • Have you purchased any of the tools or equipment you have shown me? • What is the name of that tool? • Who is the maker or manufacturer? • When was it purchased? • Did you make the decision to purchase it? • What do you use it for? • What are the benefits and features of using this tool or piece of equipment? • If you could keep only one of the tools or pieces of equipment, which one would it be?

▶ _____

▶ _____

▶ _____

TASK RECAP

▶ Did you choose one tool or piece of equipment to write about?
▶ Are the benefits and features explained in detail?
▶ Did you use complete sentences?

Now that you visited a cafeteria or a restaurant and have written your paragraph, what steps did you actually follow? • How long did it actually take?

_____

_____

_____

_____

USE WHAT YOU'VE LEARNED

You've been learning a variety of skills within the context of being a food service manager.

In review, you have successfully

- ▶ communicated problems and changes in a plan
- ▶ checked menus for accuracy
- ▶ completed and corrected information on forms
- ▶ understood expectations of another person
- ▶ scheduled and organized people to cover a work load

1. Name two other jobs that might require these skills. How might these skills be put to use?

   Example: *hospital admissions clerks communicate patients' problems to doctors and nurses*

   _____

   _____

   _____

   _____

2. Is there anywhere else you use these skills? Where?

   Example: *at home, I check the grocery list with menus before I go shopping*

   _____

   _____

   _____

3. Now that you've completed the tasks in this lesson, can you think of two new tasks at work or at home that you might try? What are they?

   _____

   _____

   _____

   _____

■■■ TRANSPORTATION AND TRADE

In the transportation and trade industry, more than 1 million new jobs are expected to open by the year 2005. The job growth is caused by changes in transportation and an increase in personal travel. Workers in this field create ways to move passengers or **freight**. They may transport things themselves, as pilots or truck drivers. Or they may arrange transportation for others, as travel agents or air traffic controllers.

SOME SKILLS YOU WILL PRACTICE IN THIS LESSON

► Prepare and Follow a Schedule
► Acquire and Evaluate Information
► Understand Systems
► Work with Cultural Diversity
► Select Technology

Shipping and receiving clerks record incoming and outgoing shipment information. By counting, inspecting, weighing, and measuring freight and packages, shipping and receiving clerks verify shipping invoices. By carefully recording shipment information, a shipping and receiving clerk tracks what goods are being sent or received by his or her employer.

Using many forms and documents, a shipping and receiving clerk may also use a computer and printer to revise shipping and receiving schedules or **log** incoming and outgoing shipment information.

SOME RELATED JOBS

mail clerk
bank teller
order filler
truck delivery salesperson

Racing Against Time

Forklifts zipping up and down narrow rows. Stock clerks shouting out numbers and items. The ProRacers warehouse, where you are a shipping and receiving clerk, has already shipped or received two orders this morning.

You are logging the most recent shipment in the computer just as another semitrailer backs to the receiving dock (truck bay).

Holding a clipboard, J.J., the driver, hops out of his truck cab and makes his way toward you.

J.J. hauls truckloads of cloth and leather for a **distributor**, Beechmont Textiles. ProRacers receives daily shipments of cloth and leather bales.

J.J. calls out, "Hey, _____. Hope I haven't thrown your whole day off. Got caught in the traffic. Looked like there was a three- or four-car accident. The highway's down to one lane."

"We'll work it out. That's the way the whole day's been. Pretty crazy. Speed Racer Apparel faxed in a 'gotta have it yesterday' order. Sending it down to sunny Daytona."

"I've got another pickup and delivery this afternoon. What time do you think I'll be out of here?"

"It won't take long. I'll have to check what else is coming and going to see when I can get you out of here. Gotta get that Daytona shipment out by four. Where's your paperwork?"

"Here you go." J.J. hands you the shipment invoice and asks, "Is the coffee fresh?"

"Made it on my break. Help yourself. I'd better get to checking your shipment if I'm going to get you out of here soon."

Because J.J. came in later than scheduled, you will need to **revise the shipping and receiving schedule**.

For an outgoing shipment, you receive a copy of the purchase order, which includes when the customer needs the shipment. Based on the schedule change, you will need to **talk to crew members about unloading needs** and **arrange to have equipment to move the shipment into the warehouse**.

When you receive an incoming shipment, you verify that the order you received is the order requested and **appropriately complete receiving paperwork**. When the paperwork is completed, you **forward all paperwork to the appropriate departments**.

Taking a second count of the cloth bales, you count, "38 . . . 39 . . . still coming up short."

Signing J.J.'s delivery log, you say, "Here you go, J.J. I'll take care of the paperwork on my end."

A shipping and receiving clerk's responsibilities may vary depending on the size of the person's workplace. Some companies ship and receive large shipments that are received in a warehouse. Other companies ship and receive smaller items.

Based on the story on page 84 and your experience, can you think of at least one task you might do as a shipping and receiving clerk?

SUMMARIZE THE TASKS

There are five tasks that you, as a shipping and receiving clerk, will perform in this lesson. *In your own words*, summarize each of the five tasks after the categories listed.

CATEGORY	TASK	ORDER	PAGE
Resources	_____	____	86
Information	_____	____	88
Systems	_____	____	90
Interpersonal	_____	____	92
Technology and Tools	_____	____	94

You may have written: revise a schedule (allocate resources), engage loading and unloading crews, identify appropriate equipment available, complete appropriate paperwork, and forward paperwork to appropriate departments (systems).

PLAN YOUR TIME

Most tasks you do as a shipping and receiving clerk depend on other tasks. To plan how you will approach this lesson, list the tasks in the order that you will complete them under the ORDER column above.

The page order of the tasks in this workbook is not necessarily the order in which you would do them. Follow the order that you decided above when you begin to work through the lesson.

THINK IT THROUGH

What other information will you need to do the tasks? • What resources? • What other people are involved?

Go to the task *you* listed as 1 and continue the lesson.

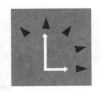

Resources: In any career, allocating and scheduling time may play a key role. As a shipping and receiving clerk, you may be responsible for revising the shipping and receiving schedule when incoming shipments are late or when priority customers request a shipment.

REVISE A SHIPPING AND RECEIVING SCHEDULE

You are a shipping and receiving clerk. You started out the day with the following schedule:

Date: Tuesday, May 15	Dock No. 1
Time scheduled	**Vendor**
8:00–8:45 A.M.	load Barrington Sporting Goods
8:45–9:45 A.M.	load McMahan
9:45–10:00 A.M.	break
10:00–11:30 A.M.	unload Beechmont Textiles
11:30 A.M.–12:30 P.M.	lunch break
12:30–1:00 P.M.	paperwork
1:00–2:00 P.M.	unload Divaria Notions
2:00–3:00 P.M.	load Karas Distributors
3:00–3:15 P.M.	break
3:15–4:00 P.M.	
4:00–5:00 P.M.	load Patriemont Racing

You don't always take your breaks at the same time. But you are supposed to take the *full hour* sometime between 11:30 A.M. and 1:30 P.M.

Speed Racer Apparel buys 40% of ProRacers' gloves and racing suits. Because it is a priority customer, its shipments go out that same day.

▶ *Speed Racer Apparel will take priority over one of the outgoing shipments already scheduled for the afternoon. When one shipment takes priority over another, you have to find out from the customer invoices when customers requested that their shipments be sent and decide which shipments can be delayed but will still be received when requested.*

For this task you will revise the shipping and receiving schedule.

VISUALIZE THE WHOLE TASK

Before you begin revising the shipping and receiving schedule, think through the steps you will need to take to revise the schedule. • What information do you need? • What other resources or paperwork will you need to complete the task? • *Remember, you can find additional resources at the back of the book.*

YOUR NOTES
How will you prioritize the shipments and revise the shipping and receiving schedule? What steps will you take to prioritize and revise the schedule?
_____
_____
_____

COMPLETE THE TASK

You can only reschedule outgoing shipments. Because an incoming shipment may already be on its way, you can't change incoming shipments. At Dock #1, you only load or unload one shipment at a time. The Beechmont Textiles shipment has just arrived at 10:30 A.M. The Speed Racer Apparel shipment will take about 1½ hours to load. To get the shipments loaded on time, you and your crews can work up to one hour overtime without notifying your supervisor.

Use the information in this lesson and the invoices on page 183 to prioritize and list the outgoing shipments for the rest of the day.

1. _Speed Racer Apparel_ _____

2. _____

3. _____

Use the Schedule on page 185 to revise the shipping and receiving schedule for the rest of the day. Allow time for breaks and lunch.

TASK RECAP

▶ Did you use the invoices on page 183 to help you prioritize the list of outgoing shipments?
▶ Did you allow time for breaks and lunch when you revised your schedule?

REVIEW YOUR PLAN

Now that you've revised the schedule, review your original plan. • What steps did you actually follow? • Did you need to delay a shipment? • Where did you find additional information?

_____

_____

Information: In many jobs, you use information from documents and forms to complete records and logs. Whether you log the information by computer or manually (on paper), you have to sort through a variety of forms and documents for the correct information.

COMPLETE APPROPRIATE PAPERWORK

Once you have received a shipment and have signed off on the deliverer's paperwork, you need to log the receipt of a shipment in the receipt log. In the afternoon, you received a shipment with a shipping **invoice** (top part of the form shown below) from Divaria Notions.

DIVARIA NOTIONS 1239 Rangeline Road Hot Springs, Arkansas 24687						INVOICE NO. 2564	
SOLD TO *PRO Racers, Inc.*				SHIPPED TO *PRO Racers, Inc.*			
STREET & NO. *180 S. 38th Street*				STREET & NO. *200 S. 38th Street*			
CITY *Provo*		STATE *UT*	ZIP *12345*	CITY *Provo*		STATE *UT*	ZIP *12345*
CUSTOMER'S ORDER *30342*	SALESMAN *K. Hansen*	TERMS *Prepaid*		F.O.B. *—*		DATE **REQUESTED** *May 18*	
30	*1 Box*	*400 ct. zippers*					
50	*2 Boxes*	*½" black plastic buttons*					
	Requested by Finishing Department						

For this task you will complete the receipt log for the incoming Divaria Notions shipment.

VISUALIZE THE WHOLE TASK

Before you begin, think of the steps you will take to complete the receipt log. • What information do you need? • What resources will you use?

YOUR NOTES

What will you do first? What steps are involved in completing a receipt log? How long do you think it will take to complete the log?

_____

_____

Using the **receipt log** below, record the receipt of the Divaria Notions shipment.

Receipt No. _43779_____   _____19____

RECEIVED FROM _____

By_____

REQUISITION NO. _____

_____

In good order the following:

QUANTITY	NO.	DESCRIPTION OF PACKAGES

TOPS FORM 3014
LITHO IN U S. A.
ORIGINAL

Sign here _____

TASK RECAP

► Were you able to find the information you needed to fill in the receipt log?
► Did you refer to the shipping invoice on page 88?

Now that you've completed the receipt log, what was different from what you had planned? • How long did it actually take? • What other resources did you use that you had not planned on using?

_____

_____

_____

Systems: Paper flow is a system. Computerization and word-processing technology have helped make paperwork somewhat easier to handle. Knowing where **documentation** can be found and where it should be returned to when completed are just two examples of how understanding a paper-flow system might help you in your career.

FORWARD PAPERWORK TO APPROPRIATE DEPARTMENTS

As a shipping and receiving clerk, you use a variety of forms and documents. Once you have completed receiving or sending a shipment, you forward various forms to the appropriate departments. How do you know which department is appropriate?

Some company policy manuals include a flowchart such as the following to show what documentation goes to which department.

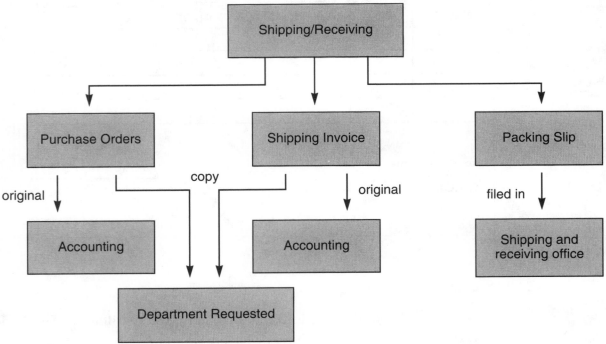

On your desk, you have a file tray for each department.

For this task you will decide which document goes to what department.

Example: An *incoming shipment* from Divaria Notions includes a shipping invoice. According to the paper flow, the original invoice is forwarded to Accounting (tray A). Because the shipment was requested by the Finishing Department, another copy should be forwarded to Finishing (tray C).

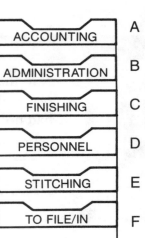

Before you begin, think through the steps you will follow to forward the paperwork to the appropriate department. • What other information do you need? • What resources might help you?

YOUR NOTES
As you sort and forward your paperwork, what will you do first? What forms and documentation will you use? How long will it take? _____ _____

COMPLETE THE TASK

Forward the paperwork to the appropriate departments. Study the flowchart. Then, using the paper file tray on page 90 and the appropriate resource pages at the back of the book, write the correct department letter (A–F) where you would file each document. (*Hint:* You will not file documents in all the file trays at this time. You may file several documents in the same file. You may file some documents in your "to file/in" tray.)

DIVARIA NOTIONS

_____ 1. **purchase order**   _____ 2. shipping invoice   _____ 3. receipt log

PATRIEMONT RACING

_____ 4. daily shipping log   _____ 5. copy of packing slip

TASK RECAP

▶ Did you use the flowchart and the paper file tray on page 90 to find the correct department for each document?
▶ Did you find the resources you needed to complete the task?

REVIEW YOUR PLAN

Now that you've sorted the paperwork to be forwarded to the appropriate department, what steps did you actually follow? • How long did it actually take?

_____

_____

Interpersonal: Many companies, when hiring new employees, ask interviewees how well they work with other people. Working as a team leader and member is one interpersonal skill that employers value highly.

SCHEDULE LOADING CREW MEMBERS

The loading schedule for today has been changed, so the crew requirements may change also. Because of the large quantity Speed Racer Apparel has requested, you will need another forklift and forklift operator available to load the **pallets**, or wooden skids, used to stack the finished goods, uniforms, and gloves.

After checking around, you find that Paul Kowalski, at Dock #5, is available during the loading time you have scheduled for the Speed Racer Apparel shipment. When you get to Dock #5, the crew chief says,

> "Paul? Sorry, he just left for the break room. When I didn't need him, I told him he could go home for the rest of the day. I bet you could catch him. I'm sure he could use the extra time. They're expecting another baby, you know. Have him let me know if he'll be putting in more time, OK?"

At the break room, you see Paul getting ready to clock out for the day. You know that Paul is a good worker, but he speaks limited English.

For this task you will develop a way to communicate:

- ▶ what work you need Paul to do
- ▶ when you need him
- ▶ where he needs to report (to his crew chief first and then to your dock)
- ▶ about how long you will need him

When you've decided what and how you are going to communicate instructions to Paul, ask a friend, co-worker, classmate, or family member to play the part of Paul.

You may use pictures, diagrams, or any form of instruction that will help you communicate with Paul. It may help to combine both written and verbal instructions.

VISUALIZE THE WHOLE TASK

Before you start, think through the steps you will need to take to develop a way to communicate with Paul who speaks limited English. • What other information do you need? • What resources might help you?

```
┌─────────────────────────────────────────────────────────────┐
│                      YOUR NOTES                             │
├─────────────────────────────────────────────────────────────┤
│  How will you begin? What forms of communication will you use? Who will you ask
│  to play the part of Paul? What steps will you take to communicate the work
│  instructions? How long do you plan to take on this task?
│
│  _____
│
│  _____
│
│  _____
│
└─────────────────────────────────────────────────────────────┘
```

COMPLETE THE TASK

On a separate sheet of paper, develop three different ways to communicate the work
instructions to Paul. Arrange for someone to role-play with you and ask the person to
give you feedback about whether your instructions were clear or not.

TASK RECAP

▶ Did you write or draw to help communicate the work instructions to Paul?
▶ Did you speak slowly enough so that a person with limited English would
understand your instructions?
▶ Did the person who played the part of Paul understand your instructions?

REVIEW YOUR PLAN

Now that you've developed different ways to communicate work instructions, review
your plan. • How long did it actually take? • What other steps were involved? • What
methods worked for you?

_____

_____

_____

_____

_____

Technology and Tools: A computer is just one type of technology or tool used in shipping and receiving. Understanding what kinds of technology and tools are used can help you perform your job more efficiently and effectively.

IDENTIFY SHIPPING AND RECEIVING TECHNOLOGY

Each company operates differently. Some smaller manufacturers have only one shipping and receiving dock staffed with one clerk alone. Some larger manufacturers have multiple shipping docks completely separate from the receiving dock. Each dock is staffed with several clerks and a supervisor.

No matter how large or small the company, either simple or complicated technology and tools are used in the shipping and receiving area. Only by observing workers in a shipping and receiving area can you fully understand how tools and technology are used. You may find:

► computers
► conveyor belt systems, or automatic guidance systems
► postage meters
► beam, digital, floor, and truck scales

Try to spend time observing a shipping and receiving clerk on the job and ask the person questions. You should call ahead to get proper permission to visit a company.

To prepare for your visit, make a list of questions to ask the shipping and receiving clerk. For example, you might ask:

► What equipment, tools, and technology do you use to ship and receive your products?
► Do you use a computer receiving log?
► What kind of problems do you have with the scales you use?
► What kinds of freight or packages does your company receive and ship?

For this task you will do two steps:

Step 1   Plan a visit to the shipping and receiving department of a manufacturing plant.

Step 2   Take a list of questions to ask that relate to shipping and receiving tools, technology, and equipment.

VISUALIZE THE WHOLE TASK

Think through the steps you will need to identify the technology and tools and their uses in a shipping and receiving department of a manufacturing plant. • What information do you need? • What resources will help you?

YOUR NOTES

How will you plan a visit to a shipping and receiving department and identify the tools and technology it uses? Write down your steps below. Include both planning the visit and how you will identify the technology and tools it uses.

_____

_____

Take the list of questions you developed to ask a shipping and receiving clerk. If you ask other questions, be sure to add them to your list.

After you have completed your plant visit, choose one tool or piece of equipment you would find useful as a shipping and receiving clerk. On the lines below, write a paragraph explaining what you have chosen, what you would use it for, and why you think it is most useful.

_____

_____

_____

_____

_____

TASK RECAP

▶ Did you remember to list additional questions?
▶ Did you write a paragraph about a specific tool or piece of equipment that you would find helpful?

REVIEW YOUR PLAN

How was your plant visit? Revise your notes to reflect how you actually identified technology or tools used in shipping and receiving. • Did you write clearly about the tool or piece of equipment and how it was used? • What else might you include in your plan next time?

_____

_____

USE WHAT YOU'VE LEARNED

You have been learning a variety of skills within the context of being a shipping and receiving clerk. Some of those skills are

- ▶ completing documents and forms
- ▶ sorting information
- ▶ working with **cultural diversity**
- ▶ prioritizing tasks
- ▶ using a log to record information

1. Name two other jobs that might require these skills. How might these skills be put to use?

_____

_____

_____

_____

2. Is there anywhere else you've used these skills? Where?

_____

_____

_____

_____

3. Now that you have completed the tasks in this lesson, can you think of two new tasks at work or at home that you might try? What are they?

_____

_____

_____

_____

U N I T   I I I

Manufacturing and Mechanical

Select Materials

Interpret a Work Order

Understand a System

Make a Site Visit

Select Tools

Office Services

Prepare and Schedule a Training Agenda

Complete an Expense Report

Create a Filing System

Talk with Clients on the Telephone

Format an Agenda

■ ■ ■ MANUFACTURING / MECHANICAL

The growth rate for manufacturing and mechanical jobs is expected to be about the same as that for all jobs over the next decade. In manufacturing firms, technical, professional, and managerial jobs will increase. Workers in this field deal with machines or hand tools to make products. Some workers help design and build the machines. Others operate or maintain the machines to create products.

SOME SKILLS YOU WILL PRACTICE IN THIS LESSON

- ▶ Allocate Materials
- ▶ Acquire and Interpret Information
- ▶ Understand Systems
- ▶ Serve Customers
- ▶ Select Tools

Cable installers are also known as outside equipment technicians or cable technicians. They work with telecommunications equipment in both homes and businesses. They install, service, repair, and remove communications equipment such as telephones, phone jacks, switchboard systems, and telephone cables.

To complete a certain job, cable installers follow work orders, diagrams, and/or customer requests. They may troubleshoot a customer's problem—faulty cables, switch outages—on-site to locate and restore proper service. A cable installer must understand various technical and organizational systems. He or she may be responsible for teaching a new technician how to perform a specific procedure such as splicing cables to an outside street telephone line.

SOME RELATED JOBS

computer equipment technician
central telephone office technician
construction contractor
inside equipment technician
electrician

Answering the First Dispatch

A cable installer may perform the same tasks during a day but is certain to find problems. That's part of the profession—solving problems—whether it's for a business owner who owns a multiline telephone system or for a residential customer whose telephone line "sounds crackly" when he calls his son in Maine.

You're beginning a day on your job as a cable installer. Using your hand-held computer, you access the main office and have a work order dispatched to you. Once you **interpret the work order**, you are ready to follow it and **make a customer site visit**.

The first dispatch of the day sends you to 4000 Corporate Way, where you are setting up a new business service for Ray Launer. Mr. Launer owns an international plastics distribution company. Judging from the work order, you are going to be at Plastix, Inc., for a couple of hours this morning. Before you leave the office, you **choose the tools you'll need** for the job and **select materials** to bring with you as well.

As you park your van, you check your watch for the time. You see a sign crew, balancing on the edges of their ladders, hanging the new Plastix, Inc., logo above 4000 Corporate Way.

Inside the new building, piles of boxes claim the territory that will soon belong to a receptionist, an office manager, and an accounting clerk.

Not seeing much sign of life, other than the sign crew out front, you call out in a friendly voice, "Hello. I'm _____

from the telephone company here to see a Mr. Ray Launer."

You hear a voice from afar. "Come on back, way back," says a man peeking over some boxes. He waves you back with a smile.

After you talk for a moment and verify the work order, Mr. Launer says, "First, call me Ray. Second, you got here earlier than I expected. If you don't mind, I'd like to get right to it. I've sketched out a basic floor plan of our offices to help you **understand our system**. I hope I'm not being too pushy, but I need my phones operational by next Monday."

You assure him, "No problem, Ray. You tell me where you want what, and I'll get it there."

Although cable installers' days are **unpredictable**, you'll find five specific tasks in this lesson. Each task is categorized as having to do with one of the following: resources, information, systems, interpersonal skills, and tools and technology.

SUMMARIZE THE TASKS

There are five tasks that you will accomplish in this lesson. Summarize the tasks by filling in the blanks.

CATEGORY	TASK	ORDER	PAGE
Resources	_____	____	102
Information	_____	____	104
Systems	_____	____	107
Interpersonal	_____	____	109
Technology and Tools	_____	____	112

You may have written the tasks exactly as you found them in the story. You may have even summarized the tasks using your own words.

PLAN YOUR TIME

The five tasks you listed above are only *part* of a cable installer's day. As you read through the story, you may have recognized a natural order the tasks might follow. Under the ORDER column above, list the tasks in the order you will complete them.

The page order of the tasks in this workbook is not necessarily the order in which you would do them. Follow the order that you decided above when you begin to work through the lesson.

THINK IT THROUGH

What other resources will you need to do each task? • What other information? • Who else is involved? • How much time do you think it will take you to complete each task? • To complete all of the tasks?

Go to the task *you* listed as 1 and continue the lesson.

Resources: Using materials efficiently begins with preparation. Wastefulness can be very costly to both the customer and the cable company. Whether you are dealing with materials that cost $10 or $1,000, you should always try to be efficient.

"Before you leave the office, you select materials to bring with you as well."

SELECT MATERIALS

Cable installers work with a wide variety of materials. As technology advances, so does the quality and, sometimes, the cost of the materials you use.

As you read on page 100, Ray Launer of Plastix, Inc., has requested an initial setup, which requires **installing** a private business line in his office. When you install any telephone line, you install a jack into which you plug the telephone/fax extension. The following picture shows the materials you'll need:

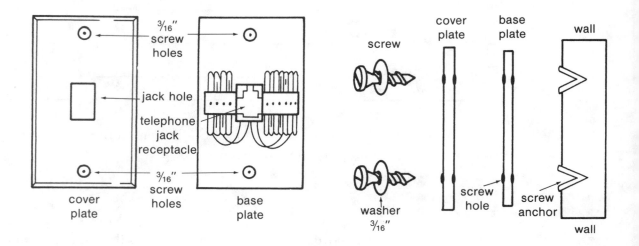

For this task you will select materials you'll need to install Ray Launer's telephone/fax jack. You will use the picture above and the toolbox on page 189 to help you complete this task.

VISUALIZE THE WHOLE TASK

Before you start selecting and calculating how many materials you will need for the Plastix, Inc., job, think through the steps you will follow. • What will you do first? • What resources will you use? • Do you need other information? • How much time do you think it will take you?

YOUR NOTES

How will you determine how much material you'll need to complete the Plastix, Inc., job? Write down the steps you will follow.

_____

_____

Use the worksheet below and the diagram on page 102 to order the amount of each material you need to install the telephone/fax jack.

WORKSHEET

Order Number _1020556_   Customer Name _____

Material(s)	Size/type	Amount
_____	_____	_____
_____	_____	_____
_____	_____	_____
_____	_____	_____

TASK RECAP

► Did you double-check your calculations?
► Did you express your answer in the appropriate measurement units?

How did it work? • What steps did you actually follow? • Did you use approximate or exact measurements? • Why?

_____

_____

_____

Information: As you know, many technical and manufacturing careers involve abbreviations and job-specific **lingo** that is unfamiliar to outsiders. Generally speaking, the more you speak and write lingo, the easier it is to understand it. Some job manuals have definitions and explanations of abbreviations and words specific to the industry.

INTERPRET A WORK ORDER

"Once you interpret the work order, you are ready to follow it."

At the beginning of your cable installer training, you were given a manual with an alphabetical listing of abbreviations, lingo, **acronyms**, etc. In your daily tasks, that reference manual is very important. You need to be able to interpret your work orders as well as other information.

Each day, your work orders are dispatched to you on your hand-held computer. Your computer screen display looks like this:

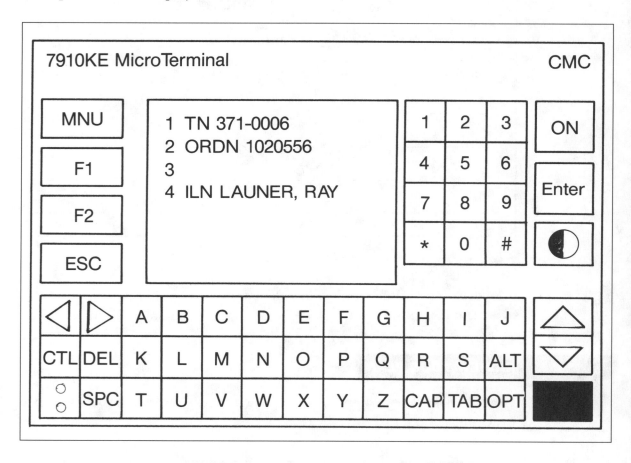

For this task you will interpret the codes on the display above. You will use the operator's codes manual on page 191 to translate these codes onto the final work order form on page 106.

Imagine that you've already copied the information from your computer display on the notepad below. This is how it might look:

	FULL WORK ORDER DISPATCH NOTES		
1	TN 371-0006	11	I1 IFB
2	ORDN 1020556	12	IFI
3		13	CA 655
4	ILN Launer, Ray	14	PR 700
5	ILA 4000 Corporate Way LK City (03330)	15	BP 5
6	ILOC Suite 6	16	TEA T145678
7	RMKS	17	$
8	RMKS Intl Stup, Instl Fx, & IFB/TTB	18	Co. Loc 398 Hamilton
9	CSTR MTNG ONST	19	
10	I1 TTB	20	

VISUALIZE THE WHOLE TASK

Before you start, think through the steps you will take to interpret the work order.
• What will you do first? • What information do you need? • Where might you find it?
• What resources would be helpful? • How long do you think it will take you?

YOUR NOTES
There's a lot of information in front of you. How will you interpret the work order? Write down the steps you plan to follow.
_____
_____
_____
_____
_____

Use your notes and the operator's codes on page 191 to interpret your computerized dispatch. Fill out the work order form below. *As a cable installer, you would normally have a whole notepad of work order forms.*

DATE _____	CUSTOMER _____
ORDER # _____	MAIN PHONE # _____

ADDRESS (CITY, STATE, ZIP)_____

C.O. LOCATION _____

CHECK ONE: ☐ FR ☐ BR   TOTAL # LINES _____

SERVICE CODE	SERVICE DESCRIPTION (NO CODES)	DATE SERVICE COMPLETED

SPECIAL INSTRUCTIONS: _____	CUSTOMER SIGNATURE: _____
_____	TECHNICIAN SIGNATURE:_____
SERVICE CODES: I = Installation R = Repair U = Upgrade M = Removal	TECHNICIAN CN # _____

TASK RECAP

▶ Did you use the manual in the back of the book to interpret the codes, acronyms, or abbreviations?

▶ Did you find and use the work order form?

▶ Did you spell the customer's name correctly?

▶ Did you include the order number?

Now that you have completed the work order form, look at your plan. • What steps did you actually follow? • What didn't you do? • What was hard? • What was easy?

_____

_____

Systems: Communications systems are all around us. Multiline telephone systems, voice mail, fax machines, and other communications equipment form a network through which information is transmitted. Understanding how each part works with other parts can help you solve problems.

UNDERSTAND A SYSTEM

A communication system may be spread across many locations and have different technologies all **interfacing** to **transmit** information. If one part of the system is removed or breaks down, communication stops.

For this task you will need to stand up, walk around, and even go outside. You are going to investigate how your telephone system works. You will find the parts to your telephone system and express how each of those parts works with and is connected to another. If you prefer, you can build a model system. *You may choose to go to the home or business of someone you know to complete this task.*

The following diagram is a picture of how a telephone system might work:

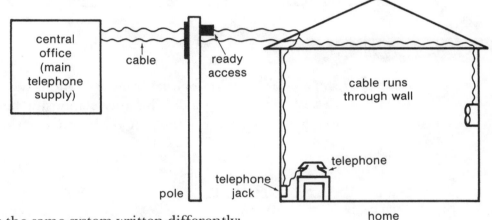

Here is the same system written differently:

Written sequence

1. main telephone supply comes from the district 5 central office

2. the local source is a ready access telephone pole 23 feet from my house

3. a cable enters my house near the roof

4. a cable runs through the wall of the bedroom and kitchen

5. I have a wall telephone mounted to a wall jack in the kitchen and a jack near the bed with a telephone

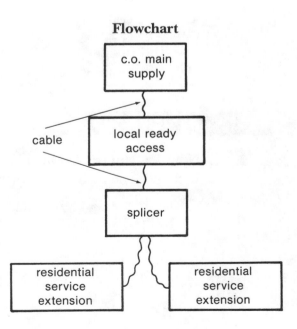

Flowchart

VISUALIZE THE WHOLE TASK

Before you jump into the investigation, take time to think through the steps you will take to understand a communication system. • Who is involved? • What will you do first? • How much time do you think it will take? • What information might be helpful?

YOUR NOTES

What steps will you follow? Write down the *who, what, when, where,* and *how* of your systems investigation.

_____

_____

_____

COMPLETE THE TASK

Locate the parts of a business or residential communications system. On a separate sheet of paper, describe in words or a drawing the relationship between each part and how they work together. Keep track of the time that you spend on this task.

Where is this communications system located?

_____   _____
company or family name   street address

TASK RECAP

▶ Did you keep track of the time you spent on this task?
▶ Does your way of describing the communications system seem clear to others?

REVIEW YOUR PLAN

Now that you've completed the task, what steps did you actually follow? • How much time did it actually take you? • Did you plan on that amount of time?

_____

_____

_____

Interpersonal: Providing efficient and friendly customer service is an important part of the job of a cable installer.

MAKE A SITE VISIT

> *"Not seeing much sign of life, other than the sign crew out front, you call out in a friendly voice, 'Hello . . . I'm _____ from the telephone company here to see a Mr. Ray Launer.' "*

The **site,** or place, where your work order must be completed is called the customer site. As a cable installer, you visit customer sites to install, repair, or remove communications equipment at the request of a customer. When you make a site visit, it is important that you listen carefully to what the customer asks.

For this task you will draw symbols on the floor plan in the places where Ray Launer needs telephone, fax, and/or modem jacks by asking questions and listening carefully. You will read through the script on page 111 and refer to the floor plan below to complete this task. *You'll need to find a partner to read through the script with you.*

Here is a sketch of the floor plan for Plastix, Inc.:

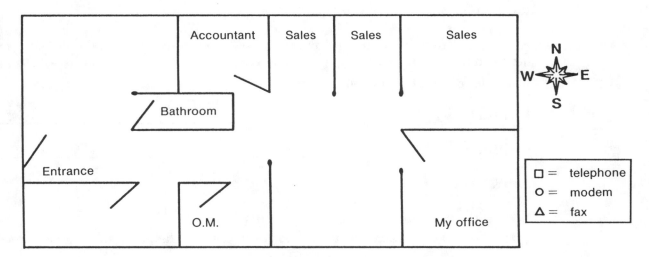

Your partner should read Ray's part in the script and should also look at the floor plan. As you read through the script, you'll use these communication skills:

▶ **feedback**—repeating information back to the customer (in your own words or using the same words)

▶ **clarifying**—asking a question to get more specific information about the customer's wants and needs

Think through the steps you will take to decide where Ray Launer needs telephone, fax, and/or modem jacks. • Who can play the part of Ray? • What resources do you need? • What other information do you need?

YOUR NOTES
How will you arrange your **customer site visit**? How much time will it take? Write down the details and steps you will follow.   _____   _____   _____

COMPLETE THE TASK

Read the script. Then draw symbols on the floor plan on page 109 in the places where Ray Launer needs telephone, fax, and/or modem jacks.

After you've decided what equipment goes where, think through the questions you asked. What feedback did you give? What clarifying question did you ask? Write one example of each type of question below.

Feedback _____

Clarifying _____

TASK RECAP

▶ Did you identify feedback and clarifying questions?
▶ Did you have the correct number of telephone, fax, and modem jacks recorded in the correct places in the office?

REVIEW YOUR PLAN

How did you do? • What steps did you actually follow? • What was hard? • What was easy?

_____

_____

SCRIPT

You: "Hello… I'm _____ from the phone company here to see a Mr. Ray Launer."

Ray: "Come on back, way back. First, call me Ray. Second, you got here earlier than I expected. If you don't mind, I'd like to get right to it. I've sketched out a basic floor plan of our offices to help you understand our system. I hope I'm not being too pushy, but I need all my telephones **operational** by next Monday. The person I talked with on the telephone said you would get my private line here in my office going today. Is that going to happen?"

You: "I have the work order and all of the materials I need to get your private line installed. I'll need to see where you want what and then decide how much time it will take to finish. I'll be happy to give you a completion date and an approximate time we'll be finished before I leave this morning."

Ray: "I told her I needed those telephones by Monday. My sales team is setting up this weekend and will be ready to hit the telephones on Monday."

You: "No problem, Ray. You tell me where you want what, and I'll get it there."

Ray: "Well, let's start back here in my office. I want my desk in the middle of the east wall here, so I suppose my telephone, fax, and modem hookup should be on that wall. I have one of those all-in-one cabinets for my computer and fax. Yeah, let's do it that way. Right outside my office I want a general office work area on that south wall, with both fax and modem capabilities."

You: "At the baseboard, toward the center of the wall?"

Ray: "That's perfect." [Facing the north wall] "I need telephone jacks in those three workspaces."

You: "Do you have a preference as to what position they are on the wall?"

Ray: "Whatever's easiest. Next to these three is my accountant's office. She'll need the same setup I have."

You: "That would be telephone, fax, and modem capabilities, right?"

Ray: "That's right. Over here on the south wall again, the office manager will need a telephone hookup."

You: "Is that the office by the west entrance?"

Ray: "Oh, no, I'm sorry, it's the second office on the south wall. The first office, near the entrance, needs both telephone and modem capabilities."

You: "Is there anything else?"

Ray: "That ought to do it. Let me know when you think you can set everything up."

Technology and Tools: For many workers, choosing the appropriate tools is a matter of efficiency and safety. Some highly specialized tools—that is, tools designed for a specific task—can be damaged and even destroyed when improperly used. When used improperly, some tools can cause serious injury to you as well as others working along with you.

SELECT TOOLS

Some tools have specific uses. Other tools are multipurpose. Hand tools are a cable installer's most valuable resource. By keeping an organized toolbox, a cable installer can avoid wasting time at a customer's site.

One year ago, you began learning how to use different hand tools. You always have your tools list on pages 193 and 195 but don't always need to refer to it. You are preparing to install Ray Launer's telephone jack. Here's where you are in the process:

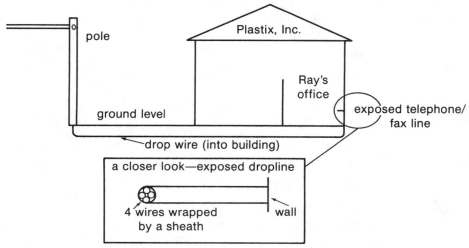

You have:

▶ run drop wire from the pole to the new office building.
▶ drilled a wire hole and two screw holes in the wall where Ray told you he wanted the telephone/fax jack.
▶ run the drop wire up the wall and through the wirehole. (The wire is exposed.)

For this task you need to select the tools to
> **Job 1: pull the sheath (protective plastic covering) off of the drop wire (cable)**
> **Job 2: connect or "punch down" the drop wire to the telephone jack**
> **Job 3: install the jack**

Before you start, think through the steps you will follow. • How will you select the tools? • What will you do first? • What other resources will you need? • What other information?

YOUR NOTES

How will you select the tools to complete the jack installation?

First, I will _____

_____

COMPLETE THE TASK

Use the wiring diagram on page 112 and the tools list on pages 193 and 195 to choose which tools you'll need to complete the task. Also look at the toolbox on page 189. On the list below, write the name of the tool you think is most appropriate for each job. In the second column, write why you chose that particular tool.

           Tools   Why?

Job 1 _____ _____

       _____ _____

Job 2 _____ _____

       _____ _____

Job 3 _____ _____

       _____ _____

TASK RECAP

▶ Did you use other resources in this book to help you choose the tools?
▶ Did you write a complete sentence to explain why you chose a particular tool?
▶ Did you check your spelling and punctuation?

REVIEW YOUR PLAN

What did you do differently? • Did you ask anyone for help? • Did it take you longer than you had planned?

_____

_____

_____

USE WHAT YOU'VE LEARNED

In this lesson, you've been learning various skills within the context of a cable installer. Some of these skills are

- ▶ interpreting information
- ▶ cross-referencing manuals
- ▶ selecting appropriate materials and tools
- ▶ understanding a system

1. Name two other jobs that might require these skills. How might these skills be put to use?

_____

_____

_____

2. Is there anywhere else you've used these skills? Where?

_____

_____

_____

3. Now that you have completed the tasks in this lesson, can you think of two new tasks at work or at home that you might try? What are they?

_____

_____

_____

4. What interpersonal communication systems do you have at work, home, or school? How do the people or parts work together?

_____

_____

_____

_____

■■■ OFFICE SERVICES

The office services industry is expected to have a higher growth rate than the average rate of growth for all jobs by 2005. Workers in this field perform administrative tasks needed to keep organizations running smoothly. They may do clerical tasks as word processors and receptionists. They may also operate and repair computers that type, print, sort, compute, receive, and send information. Some of these workers may give technical support and training to computer users.

SOME SKILLS YOU WILL PRACTICE IN THIS LESSON

- ▶ Allocate Time
- ▶ Interpret and Organize Information
- ▶ Serve Clients
- ▶ Design a System
- ▶ Apply Technology to a Task

An administrative assistant communicates, organizes, and maintains information in written forms and documents. Including typing proposals and letters, an administrative assistant may be responsible for creating documents in an organized format.

Administrative assistants also organize and maintain file systems, answer telephones, distribute telephone or fax messages, and coordinate a supervisor's schedule. When responsible for setting up meetings, an administrative assistant prepares and organizes materials for the event, which may include both packets of information as well as visual-aid materials, such as overhead projection materials and flip charts.

SOME RELATED JOBS

office manager
personnel specialist
secretary
front desk clerk
medical assistant

Home Office Hive

The marketing reps and insurance agents refer to the home office as a hive, for a good reason. With the telephones ringing, faxes coming in, and meetings going on, the buzz of the office is somewhat like a beehive.

You work in the administrative branch as an administrative assistant. Maria Trudeau is the regional manager for A1 Insurance, Inc., a commercial lines insurance company.

Your company underwrites insurance policies for businesses (for example, property and casualty insurance for a restaurant to cover fire damages). You've been with A1 for six months and have made great strides as Maria's assistant.

Today you arrive at 7:50 A.M., and Maria's already in her office. She's reviewing some letters you typed for her yesterday. You say, "Good morning, Maria. Do those letters look like you wanted them to look?"

"Good morning to you, too; and yes, they look great. I like how you centered the meeting time and details. Maybe that way they'll all be here on time and in the right place," she adds with a smile.

"Thanks. I tried to make it clear," you add. "I noticed you remembered to bring your receipts in from your New York trip. You did give me permission to bug you about those expense things, you know," you say with a grin.

Since you started working with Maria, you've become more comfortable talking and joking with her. You've learned that Maria needs to be reminded about her expense reports. So today, you'll be able to **complete the expense report** for Maria's New York trip.

The phone starts ringing before 8:00 A.M. In addition to the expense report, most of your morning involves **taking telephone messages**, sending and receiving faxes, typing letters and documents, and, last but not least, **filing the documents and forms** you've completed.

Maria has been out of town quite a bit lately and has asked you to help her with a new challenge—coordinating a training session. On her way out the door for a meeting, Maria asks you to **format the training agenda on the computer**. She explains, "I need you to **set time frames for the agenda**. Here's an example from last month's training and my agenda. I tried to give you approximate times for each topic. I'll want to go over that tonight, so leave it on the very top of my box. Thanks. If I'm not back before you leave at 5:00 P.M., have a good evening."

"You too, Maria. See you." The telephone rings and you're back to work as usual.

An administrative assistant has to be organized and very efficient with time on tasks. Because administrative assistants juggle a variety of tasks at once, they must be able to leave and come back to a task and not miss a beat. Think of this lesson as five tasks you might perform as an administrative assistant in any given workday.

SUMMARIZE THE TASKS

How would you like to work for Maria? Prioritizing and organizing your work as an administrative assistant can be critical to how well your day goes. You read about the five tasks you will perform in this lesson. List the tasks below, as they relate to the following categories. You may choose to write the tasks in your own words or as they appear in the story.

CATEGORY	TASK	ORDER	PAGE
Resources	_____	____	118
Information	_____	____	120
Systems	_____	____	123
Interpersonal	_____	____	125
Technology and Tools	_____	____	128

PLAN YOUR TIME

Is there any logical order or flow to the tasks you listed above? When did you receive the expense report from Maria? When did she hand the training agenda to you? Under the *Order* column above, list the tasks in the order you will complete them (according to the story).

The page order of the tasks in this workbook is not necessarily the order in which you would do them. Follow the order you decided above when you begin to work through the lesson.

THINK IT THROUGH

What kind of information do you need to complete the tasks? • Where might you find that information? • In what resources? • What technology or tools do you need? • Are other people involved?

Go to the task *you* listed above as 1 and continue the lesson.

Resources: Time is a valuable resource for any worker. Certain tasks may require a given amount of time, while other tasks, because of their **complexity**, may require more time. When scheduling meetings or setting agendas, an administrative assistant needs to schedule enough time for all the information to be presented.

PREPARE AND SCHEDULE A TRAINING AGENDA

As an administrative assistant, you may be responsible for coordinating meetings. Coordinating may include anything from preparing an **agenda**, or time schedule, for the meeting to creating materials to hand out during the meeting.

Maria has given you the following example of a training session from last month and made notes about some of the changes.

8:00 - 8:30 A.M.	Continental breakfast
8:30 - 9:00 A.M.	Introductions
9:00 - 9:15 A.M.	What do we stand for? (Mission statement)
9:15 - 10:00 A.M.	Who do we serve? (Corporate goals)
10:00 - 10:15 A.M.	Break
10:15 - 10:30 A.M.	What do we look like? (Corporate structure)
10:30 - 12:00 P.M.	Corporate Offices - New York/Northeast regional office
	1) administration
	2) ~~accounting~~ central accounting
	3) market research
	4) research & development
12:00 - 1:30 P.M.	Lunch
~~1:30 - 2:30 P.M.~~	*Regional*
~~2:30 - 3:30 P.M.~~	~~Corporate~~ offices (continued)
1.5 hr.	1 ~~5~~) claims processing
	2 ~~6~~) technical assistance
	3 ~~7~~) data processing (management information systems - MIS)
~~3:30 - 3:45 P.M.~~	Break (15 min.)
~~3:45 - 5:00 P.M.~~	Regional offices -
1.25 hr. **(until 5:00 P.M.)**	~~1) technical assistance~~
	4 ~~2~~) human resources
	5 ~~3~~) marketing and sales
	~~4) data processing (MIS)~~ Questions and answers

P.S. Please add a heading to the agenda.

For this task you will schedule time for the new agenda, based on Maria's notes.

Before you start, think through the steps you will take to complete the task. • What will you do first? • How much time do you think it will take? • Do you need more information?

YOUR NOTES
How will you change the schedule so you have enough time for each part of the training? Make notes about how you will complete the task.

_____

_____

_____

COMPLETE THE TASK

Use the form on page 197 to reschedule the agenda for the training session. _Your focus in this task should be on the time allocated for each topic or subject._

TASK RECAP

► Does the time period assigned allow for the topic to be covered?
► Did you check the order of the topics with Maria's instructions?

REVIEW YOUR PLAN

Now that you've allocated time for the training agenda, what steps did you actually follow? • How much time did it actually take?

_____

_____

_____

_____

Information: Organizing, interpreting, and communicating information verbally and orally may be how you spend most of your day in any job. Administrative assistants create and revise forms and documents constantly. Some examples are: reports, letters, proposals, and memos.

COMPLETE AN EXPENSE REPORT

One important task, as you read in the story, is completing paperwork. For Maria—in particular, her expense report needs to be filled out.

Maria was called to New York quickly. Not having time to get expense money in advance, Maria used her own money to finance the trip. Most companies have policies about **out-of-pocket** expenses and how they are reimbursed. For A1 Insurance, an employee must submit an expense report with receipts to be reimbursed, or paid back. The expense report includes:

- ▶ **meals**—breakfast, lunch, dinner
- ▶ **telephone**—local or long-distance calls from hotel or credit card
- ▶ **mileage**—on employee's car used for business purposes
- ▶ **cab or limousine**—rental for vehicle used for business purposes
- ▶ **tolls/parking**—toll road and parking fees
- ▶ **miscellaneous**—expenses not otherwise listed (for example, room tax)
- ▶ **disbursement authorization**—how expenses are to be disbursed to employee
- ▶ **employee's signature**—signature of employee submitting report

Because Maria travels frequently, you are responsible for completing her expense reports. She has attached the following memo to the receipts:

TO	REQUESTED BY *M. Trudeau*
SUBJECT *Expense Report-New York*	DATE *7/28*

- Due to quick notice I used out-of-pocket $

- Expenses + receipts attached from New York trip to corporate offices on 6/7. Please complete expense report + return to me for approval. Thanks.

DUPLICATE   SIGNED   *Maria Trudeau*

For this task you will use several receipts to complete Maria's expense report.

Before you begin, think through the steps you will take to complete the expense report. • What information will you use? • What will you do first? • Second? • How much time do you think it will take? • Do you need more information?

YOUR NOTES

Make notes about how you plan to complete the task. How will you decide which expense is in what category? What tool might be helpful for you to calculate the total expenses?

_____

_____

COMPLETE THE TASK

Use the form on page 199 and the receipts below and on page 122 to complete Maria's expense report.

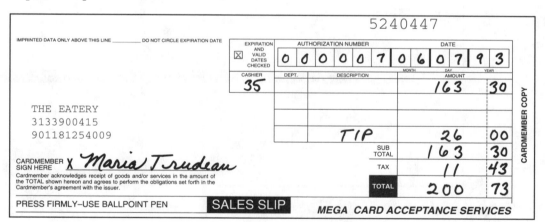

RENTAL CAR RECEIPT

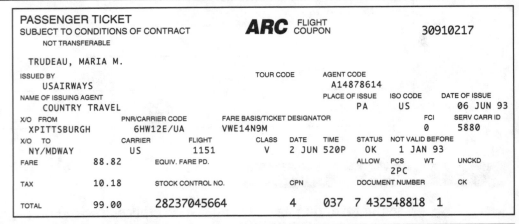

```
                                                              5240447

IMPRINTED DATA ONLY ABOVE THIS LINE ____ DO NOT CIRCLE EXPIRATION DATE
                                    EXPIRATION  AUTHORIZATION NUMBER          DATE
                                    AND
                                 X  VALID
                                    DATES
                                    CHECKED                          MONTH   DAY    YEAR
                                 CASHIER  DEPT.    DESCRIPTION              AMOUNT
                                          37    211-7480
  ACE RENT A CAR
  3133900415
  901181254009
                                                              SUB
                                                              TOTAL
CARDMEMBER X  Maria Trudeau                                   TAX
SIGN HERE
Cardmember acknowledges receipt of goods and/or services in the amount of
the TOTAL shown hereon and agrees to perform the obligations set forth in the  TOTAL   40  61
Cardmember's agreement with the issuer.

PRESS FIRMLY—USE BALLPOINT PEN    SALES SLIP   MEGA CARD ACCEPTANCE SERVICES
```

CARDMEMBER COPY

AIRLINE TICKET

PASSENGER TICKET			
SUBJECT TO CONDITIONS OF CONTRACT		**ARC** FLIGHT COUPON	30910217
NOT TRANSFERABLE			

TRUDEAU, MARIA M.

ISSUED BY		TOUR CODE	AGENT CODE
USAIRWAYS			A14878614

NAME OF ISSUING AGENT		PLACE OF ISSUE	ISO CODE	DATE OF ISSUE
COUNTRY TRAVEL		PA	US	06 JUN 93

X/O FROM	PNR/CARRIER CODE	FARE BASIS/TICKET DESIGNATOR	FCI	SERV CARR ID
XPITTSBURGH	6HW12E/UA	VWE14N9M	0	5880

X/O TO	CARRIER	FLIGHT	CLASS	DATE	TIME	STATUS	NOT VALID BEFORE
NY/MDWAY	US	1151	V	2 JUN	520P	OK	1 JAN 93

FARE	88.82	EQUIV. FARE PD.		ALLOW	PCS	WT	UNCKD
					2PC		

TAX	10.18	STOCK CONTROL NO.	CPN	DOCUMENT NUMBER	CK
TOTAL	99.00	28237045664	4	037 7 432548818	1

HOTEL RECEIPT

Holiday Star Inn

St. James and Orleans Sts.
New York, NY 00456

ROOM	378 REG# 55898
ARRIVAL	6/07/93
DEPART	6/08/93 PAGE 1
# GUESTS	1
ACCOUNT	

DATE	DESCRIPTION	REFERENCE	CHARGE	CREDIT	BALANCE
6/07/93	LOCAL CALL	37800 2668959	.50		.50
6/07/93	ROOM	37800 ROOM 378	55.00		55.50
6/07/93	TAX	37800 ROOM 378	5.50		61.00
6/08/93	LOCAL CALL	37800 2325922	.50		61.50
6/08/93	VISA/MC	37800		61.50	.00
			***** TOTAL DUE *****		.00

TASK RECAP

▶ Did you make sure you included all the expenses?
▶ Did you match the expenses to the correct day?

REVIEW YOUR PLAN

Now that you've completed the expense report, what steps did you actually follow?
• Did you use a calculator? • What did you do differently? • What was more difficult than you had planned?

Systems: In both large and small companies, systems of information are created to keep the information accessible and organized. As an administrative assistant, you may create many filing systems to store and maintain information. Whether you use computerized or manual files, a highly organized system promotes efficiency.

CREATE A FILING SYSTEM

You have been working with A1 Insurance for six months. Since you started, several things have changed with the company structure. A decision was made at the corporate level to **decentralize** some of the corporate responsibilities to regional offices. The regions divide the Continental United States into seven geographical areas as follows:

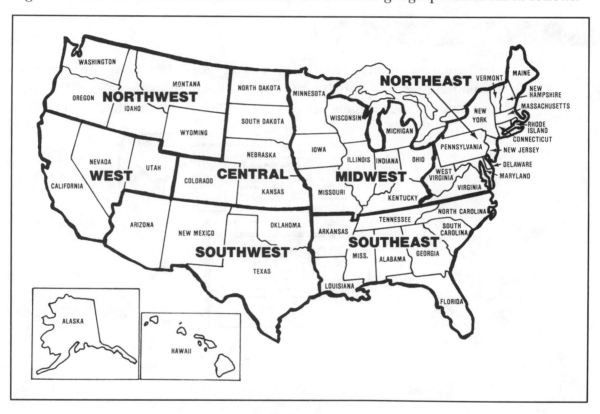

For this task you need to create a filing system that organizes information by region and then by state.

VISUALIZE THE WHOLE TASK

Before you start creating the filing system, think through the steps you will take. • What will you do first? • Second? • How much time do you think it will take? • Do you need more information? • What resources will you need?

Write down how you plan to complete this task. Which region will you start with? How will you organize the information?

_____

_____

_____

COMPLETE THE TASK

Use the map on page 123. Create a filing system by writing the names of the six remaining regions alphabetically on the file drawers on page 201. Write the names of the states in each region alphabetically. One file drawer has been done for you.

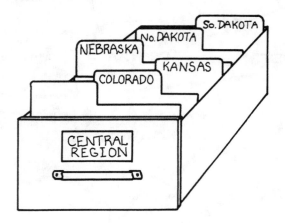

TASK RECAP

▶ Did you organize the files by region and then by state?
▶ Did you include all the states under the appropriate region?

REVIEW YOUR PLAN

Now that you've organized the filing system, what steps did you follow? • How much time did it actually take?

_____

_____

Interpersonal: Talking with clients and listening to and writing down telephone messages clearly and correctly are important parts of the role of an administrative assistant.

TALK WITH CLIENTS ON THE TELEPHONE

As an administrative assistant, one of your major responsibilities is answering the telephone. Some days, you may spend the better part of your time talking with clients as well as colleagues on the telephone. Writing down the message while talking, you'll usually need to ask questions to get a complete message.

The following message is an example of a complete message:

IMPORTANT MESSAGE

FOR __Dana Collins__

DATE __6-28__   TIME __3:40__   A.M. / (P.M.)

M __R__ __James Butler__

OF __Southwest Regional Office, P.O. Box 19__ __Reno, Nevada 00012__

PHONE __(555) 502-1432__ FAX: __(555) 577-0333__

TELEPHONED	X	PLEASE CALL	X
CAME TO SEE YOU		WILL CALL AGAIN	
RETURNED YOUR CALL		**URGENT**	

MESSAGE __Needs to talk to you about the Santa Fe conference next week. Please call tomorrow afternoon between 4-5 P.M.__

SIGNED __Anita Chung__

For this task you will role-play a telephone conversation using the script on page 126. Ask a friend or family member to be the caller, Mr. Cruz. Use the telephone conversation and additional questions you develop to complete the telephone message form for your supervisor, Maria.

For this task you will role-play a telephone conversation using the script on page 126.

VISUALIZE THE WHOLE TASK

Before you begin, think through what steps you will take to arrange the role-play and how you will get all the information necessary to complete the task. • What information do you need? • How will you arrange the role-play? • Who will help you? • *Remember, you will be completing the telephone message form and developing questions to ask to get all the information as you talk with Mr. Cruz.*

COMPLETE THE TASK

Use the telephone conversation role-play below, adding your own questions to obtain all the information you need to complete the telephone message form on page 127. It is 9:44 A.M. on July 28.

> You: Administration, Maria Trudeau's office.

> Mr. Cruz: Hello, I'm calling for Ms. Trudeau.

> You: I'm sorry, she's in a meeting right now. May I take a message?

> Mr. Cruz: Please. I'm Jack Cruz calling from Diadem Company.

> You: Is that D-I-A-D-E-M?

> Mr. Cruz: Yes.

> You: At what number can Ms. Trudeau reach you?

> Mr. Cruz: Area code (404) 555-4442.

> You: That's (404) 555-4442? What's the best day and time for her to reach you?

> Mr. Cruz: I really need to speak with her by tomorrow afternoon.

> You: Ms. Trudeau won't be back in the office until 5:00 P.M., or later. Would tomorrow morning or afternoon be better for you?

> Mr. Cruz: Early morning is better, between 8:00 A.M. and 9:00 A.M.

What information do you still need? What questions could you ask to get that information? Write them below.

_____

_____

```
┌─────────────────────────────────────────────┐
│              IMPORTANT MESSAGE                │
│                                               │
│   FOR _____ │
│                                      A.M.     │
│   DATE _____  TIME _____ P.M. │
│                                               │
│   M _____ │
│                                               │
│   OF _____ │
│                                               │
│   PHONE _____ │
│                                               │
│   ┌──────────────────┬──┬──────────────┬──┐  │
│   │ TELEPHONED       │  │ PLEASE CALL  │  │  │
│   ├──────────────────┼──┼──────────────┼──┤  │
│   │ CAME TO SEE YOU  │  │ WILL CALL    │  │  │
│   │                  │  │ AGAIN        │  │  │
│   ├──────────────────┼──┼──────────────┼──┤  │
│   │ RETURNED YOUR    │  │              │  │  │
│   │ CALL             │  │ URGENT       │  │  │
│   └──────────────────┴──┴──────────────┴──┘  │
│                                               │
│   MESSAGE _____ │
│   _____ │
│   _____ │
│   _____ │
│   _____ │
│   _____ │
│   _____ │
│                                               │
│   SIGNED _____ │
└─────────────────────────────────────────────┘
```

TASK RECAP

- ▶ Did you write a complete name and telephone number of the caller?
- ▶ Did you ask what day and time might be a good time for Maria to return the call?
- ▶ Did you ask for the fax number?

REVIEW YOUR PLAN

Now that you've completed the telephone message form, what steps did you actually follow? • What other information did you need to obtain from Mr. Cruz? • What other questions did you ask?

_____

_____

_____

Technology and Tools: Administrative assistants use a variety of office equipment and technology in their daily tasks. Computers are becoming **invaluable** in almost any office setting. The more you know about computers and how they can work for you, the better opportunities you will have in any company.

FORMAT AN AGENDA

Maria has asked you to prepare an agenda, including revising the times and **formatting** the agenda.

For this task there are two steps:

Step 1 Learn about computers and word-processing programs used by an administrative assistant.

Step 2 Use a computer to format the training agenda you revised earlier in the lesson.

Step 1 Set up an appointment with someone to learn about computers and word-processing programs. You will want to prepare a list of questions to ask, such as the following:

> ▶ For what kind of tasks do you use computers?
> ▶ What kind of computers and programs do you use?
> ▶ What can the programs help you do?
> ▶ Where did you learn how to use the computer?

Step 2 Use a computer to format the training agenda.

How will you do it? If you can't locate a computer to use, try the library. Some printing shops have computers accessible. *Remember that the purpose of creating a format for a document is to present the information in an organized, easily understood way.*

You may want to use a format similar to the original agenda. You may also choose to completely change the format, using a heading that includes:

> ▶ name of the company
> ▶ presenter's name
> ▶ date and time of the training

For example, you used the following format for the first three lines of a managers' meeting agenda for the *day before* the new employees' training.

> A1 INSURANCE, INC.
> Presenter: Ms. Maria Trudeau
> Thursday, July 14

Before you begin the task, think through the steps you will take to set up your informational appointment with an administrative assistant and then how you will format the training agenda. • How will you choose which program is best? • What other information do you need? • What resources do you need to gather?

YOUR NOTES
Write down the steps you will follow to arrange an information interview and format the training agenda. What will you do first? Second?   _____   _____   _____

COMPLETE THE WHOLE TASK

Arrange an informational interview and meet with an administrative assistant. Then, produce a completely formatted, professional training agenda.

TASK RECAP

▶ Did you choose a format that best suited your needs?
▶ Is the format easily understood?
▶ Did you double-check the agenda for accuracy?

REVIEW YOUR PLAN

Now that you've talked with an administrative assistant and completed the agenda, what steps did you actually follow? • How long did it actually take? • What did you learn that you weren't expecting?

_____ _____

_____

_____

_____

_____

USE WHAT YOU'VE LEARNED

The skills you've learned in this lesson have been within the context of being an administrative assistant.

In this lesson you have

- ▶ prioritized and organized information
- ▶ scheduled time for tasks
- ▶ used a computer
- ▶ orally communicated information
- ▶ categorized expenses

1. Name two other jobs that might require these skills. How might these skills be put to use?

_____

_____

_____

2. Is there anywhere else you've used these skills? Where?

*I categorized expenses for the family budget*_____

_____

_____

3. Now that you have completed the tasks in this lesson, can you think of two new tasks at work or at home that you might try? What are they?

_____

_____

_____

_____

ANSWER KEY

UNIT I

EDUCATION AND HUMAN SERVICES

SELECT SUPPLIES: COMPLETE THE TASK
Pages 8–9

Your supply order worksheet should look like this:

SUPPLY ORDER WORKSHEET THOMAS JEFFERSON JUNIOR HIGH		
Supply Description	**Notes**	**Total Amount**
white poster boards	10 groups × 2 boards = 20	20 white poster boards
black wide-tip markers	10 groups × 2 markers = 20	20 black markers
green wide-tip markers	10 groups × 2 markers = 20	20 green markers
green felt squares	25 students + 28 = 53	53 green felt squares

CORRECT A HOMEWORK ASSIGNMENT: COMPLETE THE TASK
Pages 10–11

Benita's corrected homework assignment should look like this:

You should also have entered Benita's score, 22, across from her name and beneath assignment #9 on the class grade book on page 12.

Benita del Marco   Assignment #9
December 12   22

1. 2.3   2. 12.37   3. 2.316   4. 3.4169   5. 11.3
    13.7   3.61   12.413   2.2134   12.6
  + 34.6   + 14.28   + 3.714   + 3.4192   48.0
   (+3) 50.6   (+3) 30.26   (0) 17.445   (+2) 9.0495   + 29.6
                                                                 (+3) 101.5

6. 7.14   7. 4.702   8. 7.4136   9. 837.42   10. 9.2
    2.47   46.843   8.2004   84.24   11.03
    36.72   18.937   9.3090   2.1   23.476
  + 84.92   9.247   6.6748   + 176.837   + 37.0009
   (+3) 131.25   + 83.201   + 5.9216   (+2) 1100.597   (0) 70.7069
                 (+3) 162.930   (+3) 37.5194

FIND AND CORRECT MISTAKES: COMPLETE THE TASK

Pages 12–13

The corrected grade book should look like this:

5th Grade NAME	#1 20 pts.	#2 25 pts.	#3 30 pts.	#4 100 pts.	#5 30 pts.	#6 30 pts.	#7 100 pts.	#8 25 pts.	#9 30 pts.	#10 100 pts.	490 pts.
E. Alexander	18	24	30	96	25	28	92	24	27	94	~~468~~ 458
D. Brown	19	25	30	98	29	29	97	24	30	98	479
J. Catron	15	21	28	86	21	20	74	23	24	80	~~382~~ 392
K. Dellinger	11	14	20	65	18	19	64	18	21	68	318
B. del Marco	18	20	27	94	24	28	91	22	22	93	439
E. Estevez	20	25	29	98	30	28	99	24	30	99	~~464~~ 482
A. Fontana	12	0	15	71	17	18	76	0	19	73	301
S. Groebel	17	22	26	88	26	25	85	24	27	90	430

INSTRUCT A STUDENT: COMPLETE THE TASK

Pages 14–15

Ask the person you instructed for feedback about your teaching session.

USE A CALCULATOR TO FIND TOTAL COST: COMPLETE THE TASK

Pages 16–17

Your completed order form should look like this:

ORDER FORM			
Quantity	**Product**	**Unit Price**	**Total**
20	white poster boards	.50	10.00
20	black wide-tip markers	1.19	23.80
20	green wide-tip markers	1.19	23.80
53	green felt squares	.29	15.37
			72.97

USE WHAT YOU'VE LEARNED

Page 18

Answers will vary.

HEALTHCARE
PLAN A SHIFT SCHEDULE: COMPLETE THE TASK
Pages 22–23

Your shift schedule might look something like this:

SAMPLE SHIFT SCHEDULE

Time	Activity	Time	Activity
7:00 A.M.	shift change	11:30	
7:15	team meeting	11:45	
7:30	Adams 355	12:00 P.M.	lunch (1 hour)
7:45	routine consult/charts	12:15	
8:00	de Vecchio #362	12:30	
8:15	discharge instructions	12:45	
8:30	charts	1:00	
8:45		1:15	
9:00		1:30	
9:15	Mundorf #350	1:45	
9:30	routine consult/charts	2:00	break
9:45	break	2:15	Mundorf #350-dressings
10:00	Lichens #368	2:30	routine consult/charts
10:15	routine consult/charts	2:45	
10:30		3:00	team meeting
10:45		3:15	
11:00	Sheehan #352	3:30	shift change
11:15	routine consult/charts		

For Step 1, the part of the patient summary record you completed should look like this:

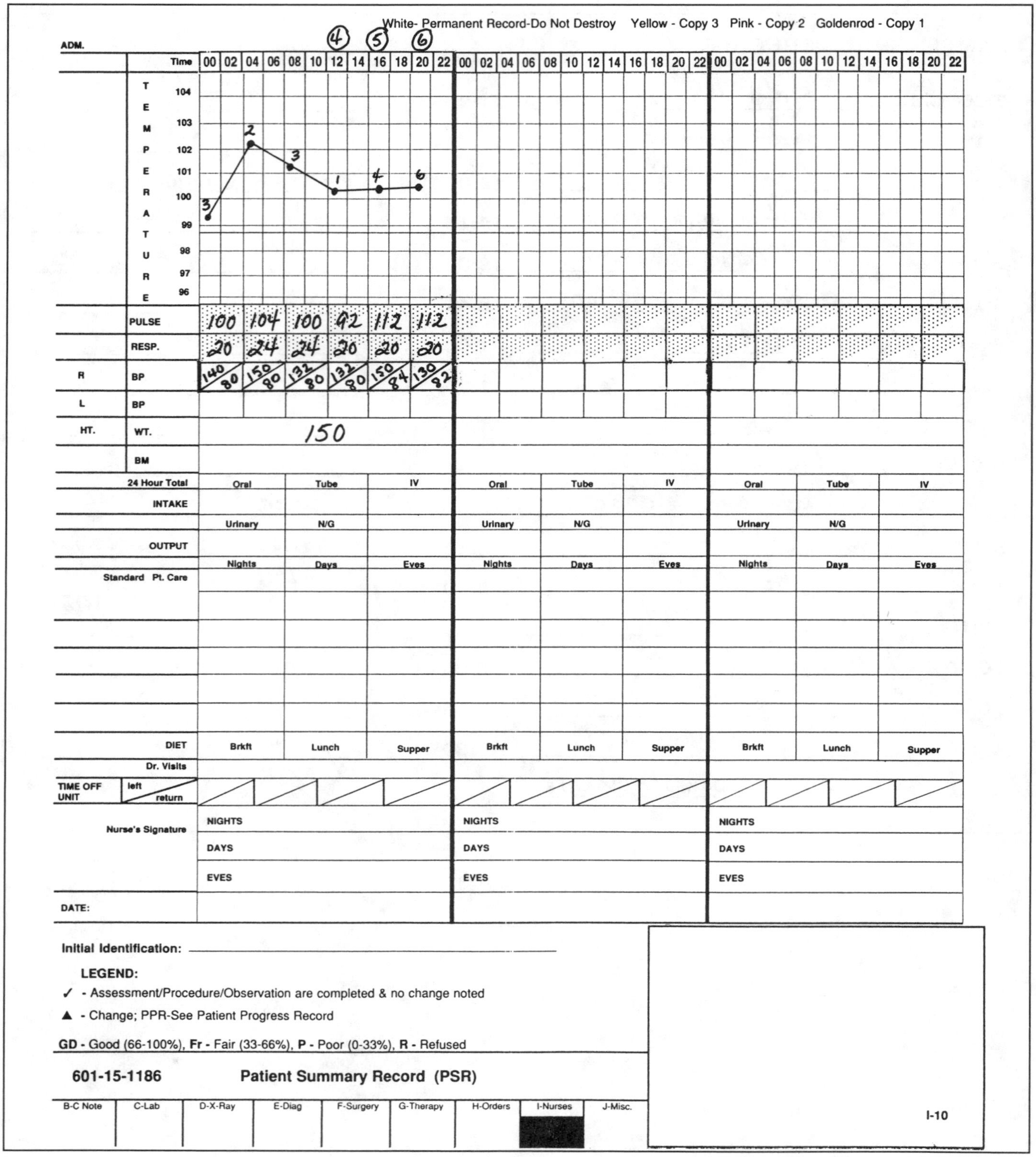

White- Permanent Record-Do Not Destroy			Yellow - Copy 3		Pink - Copy 2		Goldenrod - Copy 1					

ADM.

Time: 00 02 04 06 08 10 12 14 16 18 20 22 | 00 02 04 06 08 10 12 14 16 18 20 22 | 00 02 04 06 08 10 12 14 16 18 20 22

TEMPERATURE (104, 103, 102, 101, 100, 99, 98, 97, 96)

Plotted points: 3 at 99, 2 at 102, 3 at ~101.5, 1 at ~100, 4 at ~100, 6 at ~100.5

Circled at top: ④ ⑤ ⑥

PULSE	100	104	100	92	112	112		
RESP.	20	24	24	20	20	20		
R BP	140/80	150/80	132/80	132/80	150/84	130/82		
L BP								
HT. WT.			150					
BM								

24 Hour Total	Oral	Tube	IV	Oral	Tube	IV	Oral	Tube	IV
INTAKE									
	Urinary	N/G		Urinary	N/G		Urinary	N/G	
OUTPUT									
	Nights	Days	Eves	Nights	Days	Eves	Nights	Days	Eves
Standard Pt. Care									

DIET	Brkft	Lunch	Supper	Brkft	Lunch	Supper	Brkft	Lunch	Supper
Dr. Visits									

TIME OFF UNIT: left / return

Nurse's Signature:
NIGHTS | NIGHTS | NIGHTS
DAYS | DAYS | DAYS
EVES | EVES | EVES

DATE:

Initial Identification: _____

LEGEND:

✓ - Assessment/Procedure/Observation are completed & no change noted

▲ - Change; PPR-See Patient Progress Record

GD - Good (66-100%), **Fr** - Fair (33-66%), **P** - Poor (0-33%), **R** - Refused

601-15-1186   **Patient Summary Record (PSR)**

B-C Note	C-Lab	D-X-Ray	E-Diag	F-Surgery	G-Therapy	H-Orders	I-Nurses	J-Misc.	
									I-10

For Step 2, part of a completed portion of a patient progress record (PPR) is shown below. Your PPR from page 159 should look like this:

Date	Hour	Code	Notations
10/20/93	0900	N	Morphine 2 mg given in IVP for pain in lower left leg for pain and abdominal discomfort.
10/20/93	1100	N	Patient reported more pain after last medication given 2 hrs. ago. On a scale of 1-10, rates pain as a 7. Doctor will be notified.

UNDERSTAND A REFERENCE MANUAL: COMPLETE THE TASK
Pages 26–27
Your completed discharge instructions and referral form should look like this:

DISCHARGE INSTRUCTIONS	INSTRUCTION CARD GIVEN
Follow laceration instruction card. Keep clean and dry. Salve tonight. Take Advil for pain. REFERRED TO Name _Hospice Care_ Address _1509 Jackson St._ _Whitney, MO 87543_ Contact _Rachel Emerson_ Phone _639 – 8500_ Physician _Gregory Lambert, MD_ Nurse _Meg Samuels, RN_ Nurse's Aide _Pam Jansen_	☐ CAST CARE ☐ CRUTCH WALKING ☐ SPRAINS/SOFT TISSUE ☐ COLDS/SORE THROAT ☐ VOMITING/DIARRHEA ☐ URINARY TRACT INFECTION ☐ HERPES ☐ GONORRHEA ☐ PREG/VAG. BLEEDING ☐ LACERATION ☐ EYE INJURY ☐ ANIMAL BITE ☐ FEVER ☐ HEAD INJURY ☐ CHEST PAIN ☐ LOWER BACK INJURY ☐ OTHER

Patient Name	EU Number	Physician	Date
Angelina de Vecchio	E-284682	Gregory Lambert	11-2

EXPLAIN DISCHARGE INSTRUCTIONS: COMPLETE THE TASK

Pages 28–29

Ask the person you instructed for feedback about how well he or she understood the discharge instructions and referrals.

CHOOSE APPROPRIATE DRESSINGS: COMPLETE THE TASK

Pages 30–31

Go over your observation checklist and the responses that you received to your questions. Did you learn new information about dressing procedures done by an LPN?

USE WHAT YOU'VE LEARNED

Page 32

Answers will vary.

UNIT II

COMMUNICATION AND SALES

CALCULATE AVERAGE SALES CALL TIME: COMPLETE THE TASK

Pages 38–39

Your daily activity goals sheet should look like this:

DAILY ACTIVITY GOALS

ACTIVITY	SALES GOAL	AVG. CALL (mins.)
Product "A"	1 sale per hour	10 minutes
Product "B"	1 sale per hour	12 minutes
Product "C"	1 sale per hour	6 minutes

DEVELOP PRODUCT BENEFIT STATEMENTS: COMPLETE THE TASK

Pages 40–41

Your product benefit statements will vary. Possible statements include:

A: Our telephone service features one comprehensive bill per month. Don't you agree that one bill would be more convenient?

B: Our new photocopier will not only punch holes while making copies, but it will also sort and stack your copies for you. This will free up your sales staff's time. That would be very helpful for your company, wouldn't it?

C: Our temp service has more than 50 years of experience. We provide each customer with one customer representative to meet your needs. It sounds as if that's the kind of service you're looking for, doesn't it?

ACCESS A COMPUTER FILE: COMPLETE THE TASK
Pages 42–43

1. 5
2. 4
3. 8
4. 6
5. 7
6. 2

MAKE A SALES CALL: COMPLETE THE TASK
Pages 44–45

Key moments during the sales call include:

1. Your introduction "*Mr. Osgoode, this is _____ with Power Mowers Unlimited.*"
2. Your first question "*Do you mind telling me whether you presently own a riding lawn mower?*"
3. Your third question "*What do you like most about your current riding mower?*"
4. Your description of the new mower's warning light "*Our latest John Deere has a warning light that lights up.*"
5. Offering an appointment time "*Would two o'clock be the best time for you?*"

These key moments are described by the following:

1. using the person's name and introducing yourself and your company
2. stating the purpose of the call
3. asking survey-type questions to decide if the customer needs your product or service
4. asking what the customer likes about his or her current product
5. introducing the benefits of your product
6. negotiating an appointment time and day

LEARN ABOUT A COMPUTER SOFTWARE SYSTEM: COMPLETE THE TASK
Pages 46–47

Answers will vary. You should have listed the option you chose to have explained by a rep and the reason he or she uses this option.

USE WHAT YOU'VE LEARNED
Page 48

Answers will vary.

FINANCIAL SERVICES
ALLOCATE TIME FOR CLIENTS: COMPLETE THE TASK
Pages 52–54

Your work record should look like this:

HOURS	FOR	SUBJECT	DESCRIPTION OF SERVICES	BILLING CODE	TIME HRS 1/10
8	ABC Title, Inc. Adam Calvin in office	8:30ᴬ – Income taxes – Review Organizer	[Income tax – Business Prep]	51	2.00
9		– List of documents needed			
10	Mahoney + Hineman	10:35ᴬ –[Tax consult/projection]		52	1.50
11	∟Betty Mahoney in office				
12	Lunch Print spreadsheets	12:35ᴾ – ABC Title, Inc. [N/c office time]		80	0
1	Desirable Delectables	1:30ᴾ [Reviewed '92 financial statements]		30	.50
2	∟Cassandra Bertulucci in office	2ᴾ – [Begin income tax prep] (business)		51	1.00
3	ABC Title	– [Income tax prep business]		51	1.00
4	Marco di Francesca in office	– [Income tax prep – Personal/ Individual]		50	1.00
5	Li Ping	[Income tax prep – Personal/ Individual]		50	1.00

DIARY AND WORK RECORD 11th Week • 78th Day • FRIDAY MARCH, 1993 **19**

CALCULATE DEPRECIATION: COMPLETE THE TASK

Pages 55–57

Your depreciation worksheet should look like this:

DEPRECIATION WORKSHEET
PROPERTY A

NAME *Marco A. di Francesca*

Your social security number
505 : 55 : 1234

DESCRIPTION OF PROPERTY	COST OR OTHER BASIS	DATE ACQUIRED	RATE (%) OR LIFE	MACRS METHOD	DEPRECIATION FOR THIS YEAR 19 93
Refrigerator	600.00	5/6/93	17.85 %		$ 107.10
Air conditioning unit	1300.00	5/4/93	12.50 %		162.50
Furnace	3000.00	5/8/93	17.85 %		535.50
				Total	$ 805.10

Your Schedule E, line 20, should look like this. (The whole form is shown on page 169.)

20 Depreciation expense or depletion (see page E–2)	20	107.10	162.50	535.50	20	805.10

UNDERSTAND THE WORK FLOW SYSTEM: COMPLETE THE TASK

Pages 58–60

Answers will vary. Written response should include: Winthrop Cooke's name (person to whom the response is directed); learner's name and initials; date written; clear purpose for response; complete sentences; correct spelling.

INTERVIEW A CLIENT: COMPLETE THE TASK

Pages 61–63

Answers will vary. All appropriate blanks must be filled in. Abbreviations must be correct, codes must be complete, words must be spelled correctly.

LEARN ABOUT SPREADSHEET TECHNOLOGY: COMPLETE THE TASK

Pages 64–65

Answers will vary. Questions 1 and 2 must be filled in. Responses should be typed or written clearly. The writing sample should include three or more paragraphs. It should be clear to the reader why you agree or disagree that there is an advantage in using a computerized spreadsheet.

USE WHAT YOU'VE LEARNED

Page 66

Answers will vary.

SUMMARIZE THE TASKS

Page 69

The order given below is only a suggestion:

CATEGORY	TASK	ORDER
Resources	*schedule staff*	3
Information	*inform chef of changes*	4
Systems	*understand staff spreadsheet*	2
Interpersonal	*talk with a customer*	1
Technology and Tools	*learn about equipment*	5

SCHEDULE SERVING STAFF: COMPLETE THE TASK

Pages 70–71

To calculate table requirements:

90 guests + 10 extra = 100; 8 seats per table = 12 round tables + 4 at head table; 1 server for 2 tables = 6 servers for 12 tables + 1 server for head table. So you will need one additional server and one extra buser.

You may have added one of these four persons to the schedule as a food preparer: Laura Ayers, Montgomery Cole, Allayna Mason, or Geoffrey McDonald. You may have added one of the following persons to the schedule as a server: Luis Aquino, Stacey Devries, Tonii Kind, Kelly Peters, Joyce Redington, Leona Schmidt, Diane Smith, or David Zybko.

Your revised staff schedule should look like this:

Staff Schedule	Ladies' League luncheon
	Shift
J. Goodman	8 A.M. – 4 P.M.
G. Graham	8 A.M. – 4 P.M.
K. Rene	8 A.M. – 4 P.M.
C. Lai	10 A.M. – 4 P.M.
———	10 A.M. – 4 P.M.
M. Brown	10 A.M. – 6 P.M.
S. Chung	10 A.M. – 6 P.M.
M. Farro	10 A.M. – 6 P.M.
R. Ferrara	10 A.M. – 6 P.M.
D. Lawson	10 A.M. – 6 P.M.
———	10 A.M. – 6 P.M.

WRITE AN INFORMATIONAL NOTE:
COMPLETE THE TASK

Pages 72–74

Your note should include the following changes:

Things to do...

To: Jerome Goodman, Chef

FROM: (your name), Food Service Mgr.

DATE: July 7

RE: Ladies' League luncheon   12 PM–2 PM

Menu changes on July 9

- 90 guests
- iced tea instead of soft drinks
- steamed broccoli
- peppercorn, <u>french</u>, oil & vinegar salad
  dressings (no ranch)   Thanks,
                          your signature

UNDERSTAND A SPREADSHEET: COMPLETE THE TASK

Pages 75–77

Name	Telephone Number
Edward Bronsen	554-9871
Sue Franner	451-3749
✓Bill O'Brien	943-9328
Ken Simmons	553-5580

(Bill O'Brien requested to work 20 hours and worked only 15.)

CHANGE PLANS TO MEET A CUSTOMER'S NEEDS: COMPLETE THE TASK

Pages 78–79

Your event worksheet for food service and maintenance and setup should include the following changes:

Event Worksheet
Food Service

Company _Ladies' League_   Contact _Mrs. Margaret Lavinier_
Address _P.O. Box 351, Walnut Hills_   Phone/Fax _515-722-0232_
Event Date _July 9_   Time (begin/end) _12 PM – 2 PM_
Number of Guests ~~75~~ 90 (CM)   Budget per person _$12–15_
Style:

- o   cake and punch   o   champagne
- o   hors d'oeuvres   o   wine
- o   buffet   o   cocktails
- X   sit-down   X ~~soft drinks~~ (ABC)
- X   iced tea (ABC)   x   hot coffee/hot tea

The Menu: (ABC) steamed
Main course: chicken kiev, ^broccoli, baked potato
with choice of butter, sour cream, or both
Salad: iceberg lettuce with choice of ~~ranch~~
or peppercorn dressing   ^french or oil +
Dessert: baked apples with cinnamon vinegar (ABC)

Cost/person _$13_ x Total guests ~~75~~ 90 = Total Cost ~~$975~~ $1,170
Deposit Paid _$500_ on _June 24_
Client Signature _Margaret Lavinier_ Date _June 24_
Balance Due _$670_ on _July 5_
Sales/Catering Manager _Celeste Reed_ Date _June 24_

**Call sales/catering manager at 550-5550 with questions or problems

---

Event Worksheet
Maintenance and Setup

Company _Ladies' League_   Contact _Mrs. Margaret Lavinier_
Address _P.O. Box 351, Walnut Hills_ Phone/Fax _515 - 722 - 0232_
Room (Banquet Hall) _Van Meter_ Occupancy _120_
Date reserved _July 9_ from _9:30_ am/pm to _4_ am/pm

Equipment includes (specify type when appropriate):

- X   tables _Round (8 persons each)_
- X   chairs
- X   linens (tablecloth, table skirt, napkins) _white cloth, pink linen napkins_
- o   barware (liquor assortment, wine only, beer only) _____
- X   _head table (4 seats)/white cloth_
- o   _table skirt (ABC)_
- o   _____

Service includes:

- X   servers   o   bartenders   X   cleanup
- X   setup   o   security   o   _____

Total cost _$350_ Deposit paid _$350_ on _June 24_
Client signature _Margaret Lavinier_ Date _June 24_
Balance Due_____ on _____
Sales/Catering Mgr. _Celeste Reed_ Date _June 24_

**Call sales/catering manager at 550-5550 with questions or problems

LEARN ABOUT FOOD SERVICE EQUIPMENT: COMPLETE THE TASK
Pages 80–81

Answers will vary. Your paragraph should include the product name and manufacturer. The paragraph should be persuasive. The benefits of the equipment or tool chosen should relate to specific uses or features of the technology. Your sentences should be complete and the words spelled correctly.

USE WHAT YOU'VE LEARNED
Page 82

Answers will vary.

TRANSPORTATION AND TRADE
SUMMARIZE THE TASKS
Page 85

CATEGORY	TASK	ORDER
Resources	*revise a schedule*	1
Information	*complete appropriate paperwork*	3
Systems	*forward paperwork to departments*	4
Interpersonal	*engage loading crew*	2
Technology and Tools	*identify equipment available*	5

REVISE A SHIPPING AND RECEIVING SCHEDULE: COMPLETE THE TASK

Pages 86–87

1. Speed Racer Apparel
2. Patriemont Racing, Inc.
3. Karas Distributors

Your revised shipping and receiving schedule should look something like this:

Date: Tuesday, May 15	Dock No. 1
Time scheduled	Vendor
8:00–8:45 A.M.	Load Barrington Sporting Goods
8:45–9:45 A.M.	Load McMahan
9:45–10:00 A.M.	break
10:00–10:30 A.M.	paperwork
10:30 A.M. – 12:00 P.M.	unload Beechmont Textiles
12:00 – 1:00 P.M.	lunch
1:00 – 2:00 P.M.	unload Divaria Notions
2:00 – 2:30 P.M.	
2:30 – 2:45 P.M.	break
2:45 – 4:15 P.M.	load Speed Racer Apparel
4:15 – 5:15 P.M.	load Patriemont Racing

COMPLETE APPROPRIATE PAPERWORK: COMPLETE THE TASK

Pages 88–89

Your receipt log should look like this:

```
Receipt No. 43779                        May 15  19____

RECEIVED FROM  DIVARIA NOTIONS _____

By_____ 1239 Rangeline Rd. _____

_____ Hot Springs, Arkansas    24687 _____
REQUISITION NO.  30342

            In good order the following:
```

QUANTITY	NO.	DESCRIPTION OF PACKAGES
30	1	Box 400 ct. zippers
50	2	Boxes ½" black plastic buttons

TOPS FORM 3014
LITHO IN U S. A.   Sign here _____
ORIGINAL

FORWARD PAPERWORK TO APPROPRIATE DEPARTMENTS: COMPLETE THE TASK

Pages 90–91

1. A, C
2. A, C
3. F
4. A, B
5. F

SCHEDULE LOADING CREW MEMBERS: COMPLETE THE TASK

Pages 92–93

Answers will vary. You may have drawn a diagram or written instructions. You should have instructed Paul to: operate a forklift to load pallets for a Speed Racer Apparel shipment; be at Dock #1 at a specific time (of your choice) to load the shipment; be available for about 1½ hours; report to his crew chief before reporting to Dock #1.

IDENTIFY SHIPPING AND RECEIVING TECHNOLOGY: COMPLETE THE TASK

Pages 94–95

Answers will vary. You may have asked questions such as: Do you use computers in your area? How do computers help you on the job? What procedure do you follow to receive a shipment? To send a shipment? What kinds of scales do you use to weigh packages? To weigh truck shipments?
Your paragraph should explain what technology you see as most beneficial in shipping and receiving. You should write clearly about how specific features promote efficient work. Be sure to check all spelling, punctuation, and grammar for accuracy.

USE WHAT YOU'VE LEARNED

Page 96

Answers will vary.

UNIT III

MANUFACTURING AND MECHANICAL

SUMMARIZE THE TASKS

Page 101

The tasks must be listed as they are below. You may
have chosen a different order in which to complete
the tasks; the order given is only a suggestion.

CATEGORY	TASK	ORDER
Resources	*select materials*	4
Information	*interpret a work order*	2
Systems	*understand a system*	1
Interpersonal	*make a site visit*	3
Technology and Tools	*select tools*	5

SELECT MATERIALS: COMPLETE THE TASK

Pages 102–103

Your worksheet should look something like this:

WORKSHEET

Order Number _1020556_   Customer Name _Launer, Ray_

Material(s)	Size/type	Amount
Jack - base plate + cover plate	—	1
screws	3/16 "	2
washers	3/16 "	2
screw anchors	3/16 "	2

INTERPRET A WORK ORDER: COMPLETE THE TASK

Pages 104–106

Your completed work order form should look
something like this:

DATE _today's date_	CUSTOMER _Launer, Ray_
ORDER # _1020556_	MAIN PHONE # _____

ADDRESS (CITY, STATE, ZIP) _4000 Corporate Way, Ste 6, Lake City 03330_

C.O. LOCATION _398 Hamilton_

CHECK ONE: ☐ FR ☐ BR   TOTAL # LINES _____

SERVICE CODE	SERVICE DESCRIPTION (NO CODES)	DATE SERVICE COMPLETED
I	Initial setup, install fax, 1 private business line with touch tone base	

SPECIAL INSTRUCTIONS _____

customer meeting on site

SERVICE CODES: I = Installation   R = Repair
U = Upgrade   M = Removal

CUSTOMER SIGNATURE: _____

TECHNICIAN SIGNATURE: _____

TECHNICIAN CN # _1572_

UNDERSTAND A SYSTEM: COMPLETE THE TASK

Pages 107–108

Answers will vary. You should have listed the
company or family name and street address you
analyzed. You should have clearly shown in words or
in a drawing the relationship between the parts of a
system. You should also have tracked and recorded
the amount of time you spent working on this task.

MAKE A SITE VISIT: COMPLETE THE TASK

Pages 109–110

Your floor plan may look like the one that follows. If
you drew a floor plan using codes or symbols, be
sure you provided a key that gives the meaning of
each code.

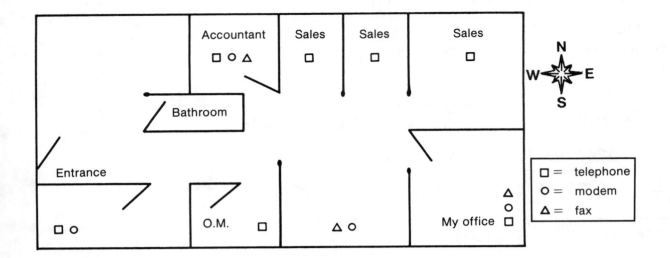

Possible examples of feedback you may have given:
- "I'll be happy to give you a completion date and an approximate time we'll be finished before we leave this morning."
- You assure him, "No problem, Ray. You tell me where you want what, and I'll get it there."

Possible kinds of clarifying questions you may have asked:
- "Do you have a preference as to what position they are on the wall?"
- "Is that the office by the west entrance?"
- "At the baseboard, toward the center of the wall?"

SELECT TOOLS: COMPLETE THE TASK
Pages 112–113

Your choice of tools should match the tools listed below. Your description of why you used each tool may vary.

	Tool	Why?
Job 1	Gas pliers	They are used to pull sheath off of drop wire.
Job 2	Punch-down tool	It is used to connect or "punch down" drop wire to telephone jack.
Job 3	Screwdriver	It is used to screw screws into wall.

USE WHAT YOU'VE LEARNED
Page 114

Answers will vary.

OFFICE SERVICES

SUMMARIZE THE TASKS
Page 117

This is a suggestion for how you may have
summarized and ordered the tasks:

CATEGORY	TASK	ORDER
Resources	*prepare and schedule a training session*	4
Information	*complete an expense report*	2
Systems	*create a filing system*	3
Interpersonal	*talk with clients over the telephone*	1
Technology and Tools	*format a training agenda*	5

PREPARE AND SCHEDULE A TRAINING AGENDA: COMPLETE THE TASK
Pages 118–119

Your training agenda should look like this:

AGENDA

Time (mins.)	Time period	Subject
(30)	8:00–8:30 AM	Continental breakfast
(30)	8:30–9:00 AM	Introductions
(15)	9:00–9:15	Mission
(45)	9:15–10:00	Corporate goals
(15)	10:00–10:15	Break
(15)	10:15–10:30	Corporate structure
(90)	10:30 AM–12:00 PM	Corporate offices
(90)	12:00 PM–1:30 PM	Lunch
(90)	1:30–3:00	Regional offices (1, 2, 3)
(15)	3:00–3:15	Break
(75)	3:15–4:30	Regional offices (4, 5)
(30)	4:30–5:00	Questions and answers

EXPENSE REPORT

TRIP _New York_

Date	Breakfast	Lunch	Dinner	Phone	Amount
6/7	6.50	17.89	200.73	.50	225.62
6/8	O	O	O	.50	.50
Totals					226.12

OTHER EXPENSES (Standard forms or receipts must be attached to receive reimbursement)

Mileage × .25	O
Hotel/Motel	55.00
Cab Fare/Rental Car	40.61
Tolls	O
Parking	O
Airline Tickets	99.00
Micellaneous	5.50 (room tax)
Total Expenses	426.23
Less Advance	O
Amount Due Employee	426.23

I request and hereby authorize that the amount be disbursed in the following manner:

1. Payroll _____   Employee's Signature

2. Cash Payment _____   _____

3. Other (specify) _____   Supervisor's Signature

_____

CREATE A FILING SYSTEM: COMPLETE THE TASK
Pages 123–124

Your files should look like this:

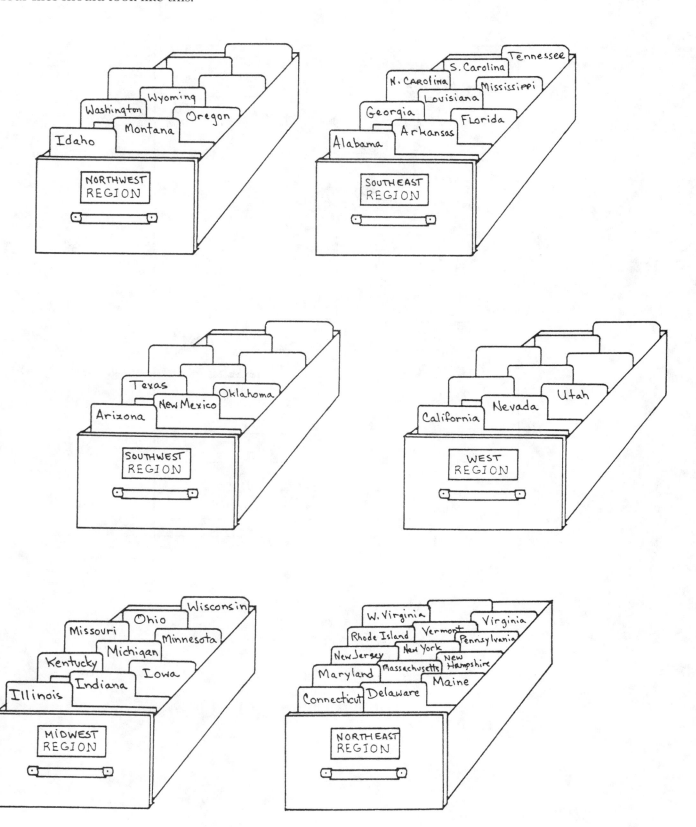

Your telephone message form should look like this:

IMPORTANT MESSAGE

FOR _Maria Trudeau_

DATE _July 28_ TIME _9:44_ (A.M.) P.M.

M _Jack Cruz_

OF _Diadem Co._

PHONE _404-555-4442_

TELEPHONED	X	PLEASE CALL	X
CAME TO SEE YOU		WILL CALL AGAIN	
RETURNED YOUR CALL		URGENT	

MESSAGE _Needs to talk with you tomorrow. He'll be in between 8 and 9 A.M._

_____

_____

_____

SIGNED _____

FORMAT AN AGENDA: *COMPLETE THE TASK*
Pages 128–129

Formats will vary. Your agenda may look something
like this:

A1 INSURANCE, INC.

Presenter: Ms. Maria Trudeau

Thursday, July 28

8:00- 8:30 A.M.   Continental breakfast

8:30- 9:00 A.M.   Introductions

9:00- 9:15 A.M.   What do we stand for? (Mission statement)

9:15- 10:00 A.M.   Who do we serve? (Corporate goals)

10:00- 10:15 A.M. Break

10:15- 10:30 A.M. What do we look like? (Corporate structure)

10:30- 12:00 P.M. Corporate Office—New York/Northeast regional office
                   1) administration
                   2) central accounting
                   3) market research
                   4) research and development

12:00- 1:30 P.M.   Lunch

1:30- 3:00 P.M.   Regional offices
                   1) claims processing
                   2) technical assistance
                   3) data processing (Management Information Systems—MIS)

3:00- 3:15 P.M.   Break

3:15- 4:30 P.M.   Regional offices (continued)
                   4) human resources
                   5) marketing and sales

4:30-5:00 P.M.   Questions and Answers

USE WHAT YOU'VE LEARNED
Page 130

Answers will vary.

GLOSSARY

abbreviations: shortened form of words or phrases used in place of the whole

accessing: opening a computer file

acronyms: words formed from the letters or syllables in a name or phrase

agenda: a list of items of business to be considered at a meeting

appropriate: especially suitable or fitting

busers: persons employed by a restaurant to remove dirty dishes or to set tables

clarifications: questions asked to make things or ideas clearer or easier to understand

commissions: fees paid to agents or employees for making a sale or providing a service

compensation: payment in the form of salary or wages

complexity: level of difficulty

comprehensive: including much or all; full

cultural diversity: differences in people's ethnic customs, language, or life-style

data processors: persons who input, or enter, information on a computer

decentralize: to scatter or spread out among various regional or local authorities

deductible: amount that can be subracted from the total

depletion: state of being used up, or out of resources

depreciation: a decline in the monetary value of an item

disbursement: payment of funds

distributor: an agent or acency for marketing goods

documentation: paperwork showing proof that an order has been placed

exemption: the act of being freed from some condition or requirement that others must meet

feedback: an oral or a written response about the value, effect, or result of an action

flexible: readily changed

formatting: preparing the way information is set up in a file or on a printed page

freight: goods or cargo carried by ship, train, truck, or airplane

installing: setting up for use or service

interest: money earned on invested capital; the amount paid to borrow money

interfacing: connecting or communicating with others

invaluable: highly esteemed; of great use or service

invoice: a bill given to a business when it makes a purchase

lingo: language that is specific to a particular job or industry

log: write down or record

maneuvers: moves or acts skillfully

modem: a device that enables a computer to transmit information over a telephone line

negotiating: discussing with others to bring about an agreement

operational: able to work or function

out-of-pocket: paid for by an employee

packing slip: a small form accompanying a shipment that includes the shipping date, shipper's name, address, and phone number, customer's name, address, order number, date requested, method of shipment, packer's name, and quantity of items ordered

patient progress record (PPR): the form a doctor fills out about a patient's condition, treatment, response, and discharge instructions

patient summary record (PSR): a chart for recording a patient's vital signs, such as temperature, pulse, respiratory rate, and blood pressure

personnel: the department that handles the hiring and firing of employees, and explaining company benefits and policies

potential: possible; something that can develop or become actual

psychologist: a specialist who has studied the human mind and behavior and treats individuals and groups who experience mental problems

prioritizing: putting in order of importance

priority: a condition of being given attention before others

purchase order: a form that someone fills out to buy equipment or supplies

receipt log: a form filled out when a shipment arrives that includes the number of packages received, the number that should have been delivered, and the condition of the shipment

reconciliation: an adjustment of differences in number amounts

referral: the act of guiding someone to a person or place for treatment, help, advice, or information

representative: a person who stands in or acts for another, especially through delegated authority

royalty: profit claimed by an owner for allowing another to rent or use a property

software: the set of instructions, including the program, operating systems, device drivers, and applications, that make a computer perform tasks

spreadsheets: forms generated on a computer that have several columns of numbers

tax organizer: a form used by a person to record financial information to determine the amount of money owed to the government on money earned or for property owned

tax return: an official document persons fill out to show how much money they owe the government or the amount of refund the government owes to them

transactions: exchange of services between persons in business or social situations

transmit: to send

unpredictable: not able to tell in advance what might happen

vendor: a company that sells products or services

SHIFT SCHEDULE

7:00 A.M.	_shift change_	11:30	_____
7:15	_team meeting_	11:45	_____
7:30	_____	12:00 P.M.	_____
7:45	_____	12:15	_____
8:00	_____	12:30	_____
8:15	_____	12:45	_____
8:30	_____	1:00	_____
8:45	_____	1:15	_____
9:00	_____	1:30	_____
9:15	_____	1:45	_____
9:30	_____	2:00	_____
9:45	_____	2:15	_____
10:00	_____	2:30	_____
10:15	_____	2:45	_____
10:30	_____	3:00	_team meeting_
10:45	_____	3:15	_____
11:00	_____	3:30	_shift change_
11:15	_____		

	CODE:					
	CPN Cardiopulmonary/Neurology		D Dietary		PT Physical Therapy	
	RX Pharmacy		OT Occupational Therapy		PC Pastoral Care	
	X X-Ray		HC Home Health Care		NM Nuclear Medicine	
	SS Social Service		ET Enterostomy		CR Cardiac Rehab	
	ST Speech Therapist		AD Audiology		N Nursing	

Date	Hour	Code	Notations
10/20/93	0900	N	Morphine 2mg given in IVP for pain in lower left leg for pain and abdominal discomfort.

* This record is intended as a statement of the patient's progress or lack of progress. If no further notation appears it means the patient received standard care in relation to the medical orders and no unusual observations were made and no unusual activities or incident occurred.

768-53-491   Patient Progress Record

I-70

B-C Note	C-Lab	D-X-Ray	E-Diag	F-Surgery	G-Therapy	H-Orders	I-Nurses	J-Misc.

Reference Manual
SOCIAL SERVICES DEPARTMENT

I.   Hospice Care   Contact: Rachel Emerson
     1509 Jackson Street   Phone: 639-8500
     Whitney, MO 87543
          A.   *Home Health Care*
               1. bedside care
               2. nutrition and food preparation
               3. general care

II. Center for Mental Health   Contact: Lisa Parry
     2020 Central Drive   Phone: 640-9000
     Denton, MO 87432
          A.   *Alcohol and Drug Programs*
               1. men's group counseling
               2. women's group counseling
               3. individual counseling
               4. family counseling
          B.   *Life Management Programs*
               1. 30 days
               2. 60 days
               3. 90 days

Customer Indicator and Product Feature List

A: *You're a telemarketing rep selling telephone services.*

Customer: "I want one bill. I have enough trouble reading the bills, let alone having two of them."

Indicator
wants less paperwork
wants billing simplified

Product Feature
- single, **comprehensive** billing

Benefit Statement: _____

_____

B. *You're a telemarketing rep selling photocopiers.*

Customer: "The sales team puts proposals in three-ring binders. It takes a lot of time. They spend hours stapling, sorting, collating, and punching holes."

Indicator
wants sales staff spending more time
selling and less time hole punching
and collating proposals

Product Features
- adjustable hole-punch settings
- programmable sorting and stacking

Benefit Statement: _____

_____

C. *You're a telemarketing rep for a temporary secretarial and administrative assistance service.*

Customer: "Our current temporary service does a great job. When we have a problem, someone from their shop works it out immediately."

Indicator
wants reliability and quick
response, good customer service

Product Features
- over 50 years of experience in temporary service
- one customer rep for each customer account

Benefit Statement: _____

_____

TELEMARKETING ROLE-PLAY SCRIPT

Mr. Osgoode: "Hello?"

You: "Good morning. Is Mr. Osgoode there?"

Mr. Osgoode: "This is Mr. Osgoode."

You: "Mr. Osgoode, this is _____ with Power Mowers Unlimited. I'm calling homeowners in your area to see how we can best meet their needs. It'll only take a minute. Do you mind telling me whether you presently own a riding lawn mower?"

Mr. Osgoode: "Well, yes, we do."

You: "Oh, fine. May I ask what type and make it is?"

Mr. Osgoode: "Let's see. We bought it 10 years ago. It's an older John Deere. May I ask what this is for?"

You: "Sure, Mr. Osgoode. At Power Mowers Unlimited we carry various kinds of lawn equipment, including riding mowers like the John Deere you currently own. What do you like most about your current riding mower?"

Mr. Osgoode: "Quite honestly, it's been quite reliable. I like the adjustable blade. I've noticed it's using quite a bit of oil lately. I think we've plain worn the thing out."

You: "John Deere is a well-respected name. I'm proud to say we carry the newest John Deere riding mower. You said *we've* worn the thing out . . ."

Mr. Osgoode: "My sons do the lawn work most of the time. Of course, I always check the oil before I start her up. I'm not sure the boys always remember."

You: "Our latest John Deere has a warning light that lights up when your oil is low. That would be helpful, wouldn't it?"

Mr. Osgoode: "Well, I suppose it would be. All those new mowers have all the bells and whistles. It sure would be convenient."

You: "After talking with you, Mr. Osgoode, I feel that you have a need to know more about the new John Deere riding mower. I have a brochure I'd be happy to send to you. But, with your permission, rather than waiting for the mail, I can have one of our service agents stop by this afternoon so you can take a quick look at the new brochure. And, because I know your time is valuable, if you have any questions, he'll be right there to answer them. Would two o'clock be the best time for you?"

Mr. Osgoode: "I'm going to the golf course at three. You could just send me the brochure."

You: "According to the service schedule, Devon Myer will be the agent in your area at two o'clock this afternoon. I'll make sure that he has the information on the new John Deere mowers, and that he knows you have a three o'clock tee time. I enjoyed talking with you, Mr. Osgoode. Thank you for talking with me today."

Mr. Osgoode: "Well, you're welcome, _____."

You: "Have a nice day. And enjoy your golf game, Mr. Osgoode."

Kind and Location of Property [_____]

TSJ [ ]   State [ ]

	Current Year	Prior Year
Number of days property rented at fair market value	7	
Number of days the property was used personally.		N/A
What percentage of the property do you own if not 100%?		

Income and Expenses

	Current Year	Prior Year
Rental income	7,000	
Non−depletable royalty income	—	
Other income: _____	—	
Advertising	65	
Auto and travel	—	
Bad debts	—	
Cleaning and maintenance	680	
Commissions.	—	
Insurance	820	
Legal and other professional fees	210	
Interest − mortgage paid to financial institutions	—	
Interest − mortgage paid to individuals	—	
Interest − other	—	
Management fees		
Repairs − carpentry and screens	115	
Repairs − electrical and plumbing	375	
Repairs − painting and decorating	230	
Repairs − roofing.	—	
Repairs − miscellaneous	160	
Supplies.	—	
Taxes	2,800	
Utilities	2,400	
Other expenses: _____		
_____		
_____		

Property and Equipment

Acquisitions − Description	Date Acquired	Cost
AIR CONDITIONING UNIT	5 : 4 : 93	1,300
REFRIGERATOR	5 : 6 : 93	600
FURNACE	5 : 8 : 93	3,000

Dispositions − Description	Date Acquired	Cost	Date Sold	Selling Price
	: :		: :	
	: :		: :	

Forms E-1, E-2, D-2, DP-1 and DP-2

201081 10-02-92

Master Tax Guide Depreciation Table

Table 3. General Depreciation System
Applicable Depreciation Method: 200 or 150 Percent
Declining Balance Switching to Straight Line
Applicable Recovery Periods: 3, 5, 7, 10, 15, 20 years
Applicable Convention: Mid-quarter (property placed in service in
second quarter)

If the Recovery Year is:	3-year	5-year	7-year	10-year	15-year	20-year
			the Depreciation Rate is:			
1	41.67	25.00	17.85	12.50	6.25	4.688
2	38.89	30.00	23.47	17.50	9.38	7.148
3	14.14	18.00	16.76	14.00	8.44	6.612
4	5.30	11.37	11.97	11.20	7.59	6.116
5		11.37	8.87	8.96	6.83	5.658
6		4.26	8.87	7.17	6.15	5.233
7			8.87	6.55	5.91	4.841
8			3.33	6.55	5.90	4.478
9				6.56	5.91	4.463
10				6.55	5.90	4.463
11				2.46	5.91	4.463
12					5.90	4.463
13					5.91	4.463
14					5.90	4.463
15					5.91	4.462
16					2.21	4.463
17						4.462
18						4.463
19						4.462
20						4.463
21						1.673

1 Control number		OMB No. 1545-0008								

2 Employer's name, address, and ZIP code	6 Statutory employee	Deceased	Pension plan	Legal rep.	942 emp.	Subtotal	Deferred compensation	Void

7 Allocated tips | 8 Advance EIC payment

9 Federal income tax withheld | 10 Wages, tips, other compensation

| 3 Employer's identification number | 4 Employer's state I.D. number | 11 Social security tax withheld | 12 Social security wages |

| 5 Employee's social security number | | 13 Social security tips | 14 Medicare wages and tips |

| 19 Employee's name, address, and ZIP code | 15 Medicare tax withheld | 16 Nonqualified plans |

17 See Instrs. for Form W-2 | 18 Other

| 20 | 21 | 22 Dependent care benefits | 23 Benefits included in Box 10 |

| 24 State income tax | 25 State wages, tips, etc. | 26 Name of state | 27 Local income tax | 28 Local wages, tips, etc. | 29 Name of locality |

Copy D For Employer   Department of the Treasury—Internal Revenue Service

Form **W-2 Wage and Tax Statement 1992** (Rev. 4-92)

For Paperwork Reduction Act Notice and instructions for completing this form, see separate instructions.

SCHEDULE E
(Form 1040)

Department of the Treasury
Internal Revenue Service   (0)

Supplemental Income and Loss
(From rental real estate, royalties, partnerships, estates, trusts, REMICs, etc.)
► Attach to Form 1040 or Form 1041.
► See Instructions for Schedule E (Form 1040).

OMB No. 1545-0074

1992

Attachment
Sequence No. **13**

Name(s) shown on return

Your social security number

Part I	Income or Loss From Rental Real Estate and Royalties Note: *Report income and expenses from the rental of personal property on **Schedule C** or **C-EZ**. Report farm rental income or loss from **Form 4835** on page 2, line 39.*

				Yes	No
1	Show the kind and location of each **rental real estate property:**	**2** For each rental real estate property listed on line 1, did you or your family use it for personal purposes for more than the greater of 14 days or 10% of the total days rented at fair rental value during the tax year? (See page E-1.)			
A	....		**A**		
B	....		**B**		
C	....		**C**		

Income:

			Properties			**Totals**
			A	**B**	**C**	(Add columns A, B, and C.)
3	Rents received	**3**				**3**
4	Royalties received	**4**				**4**

Expenses:

5	Advertising	**5**				
6	Auto and travel (see page E-2) .	**6**				
7	Cleaning and maintenance . . .	**7**				
8	Commissions	**8**				
9	Insurance	**9**				
10	Legal and other professional fees	**10**				
11	Management fees	**11**				
12	Mortgage interest paid to banks, etc. (see page E-2)	**12**				**12**
13	Other interest	**13**				
14	Repairs	**14**				
15	Supplies	**15**				
16	Taxes	**16**				
17	Utilities	**17**				
18	Other (list) ►.....................	**18**				
19	Add lines 5 through 18	**19**				**19**
20	Depreciation expense or depletion (see page E-2)	**20**				**20**
21	Total expenses. Add lines 19 and 20	**21**				
22	Income or (loss) from rental real estate or royalty properties. Subtract line 21 from line 3 (rents) or line 4 (royalties). If the result is a (loss), see page E-2 to find out if you must file **Form 6198** . .	**22**				
23	Deductible rental real estate loss. **Caution:** *Your rental real estate loss on line 22 may be limited. See page E-3 to find out if you must file **Form 8582** . . . .*	**23**	(	) (	) (	)	
24	**Income.** Add positive amounts shown on line 22. **Do not** include any losses					**24**
25	**Losses.** Add royalty losses from line 22 and rental real estate losses from line 23. Enter the total losses here				**25**	(	)
26	Total rental real estate and royalty income or (loss). Combine lines 24 and 25. Enter the result here. If Parts II, III, IV, and line 39 on page 2 do not apply to you, also enter this amount on Form 1040, line 18. Otherwise, include this amount in the total on line 40 on page 2					**26**

For Paperwork Reduction Act Notice, see Form 1040 instructions.   Cat. No. 11344L   Schedule E (Form 1040) 1992

WORK FLOW FOR DUNN'S PUBLIC ACCOUNTING SERVICE, INC.

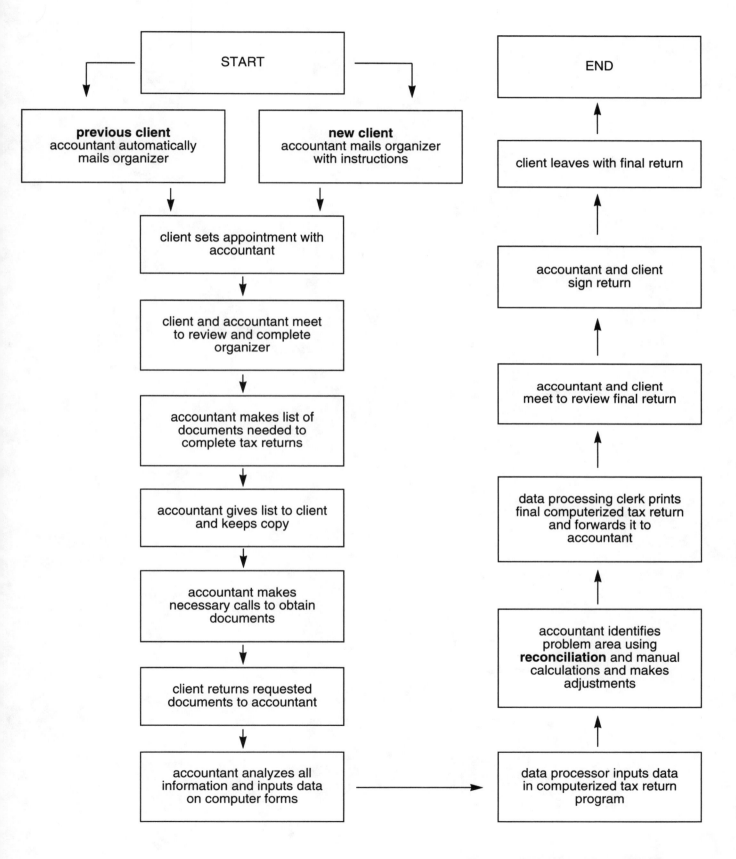

Personal Information

Y - Yes   N- No

	First Name and Initial	Last Name	Social Security Number	Presidential Election Contribution
Taxpayer				
Spouse				

	Occupation	Age on 12/31	X if Blind	Date Deceased Mo Da Yr	X if Dependent of Another
Taxpayer					
Spouse					

Present Mailing Address

Street address . . . . .   Apartment number

City of residence . . .

State abbreviation . . .   ZIP code

Dependents

Name of child living with you that is claimed as a dependent on someone else's tax return . . . .

Year or years for which a release of claim to exemption is given for a dependent child not living with you . . . .

Federal tax regulations require children 1 year of age or older to have a social security number.

C – Dependent child living with taxpayer
O – Other dependents
N – Dependent child not living with taxpayer

XN – Dependent child not living with taxpayer and release of claim to exemption should be filed
E – Child qualifying you for earned income credit (household member, not a dependent)

Did dependent have over $2300 income?

TSJ	State	First Name, Initial and Last Name	Social Security Number	Age	Relationship	Months Lived in Your Home	X if Disabled	Y/N	Code

Wages and Salaries

Please enclose all copies of your current year Forms W-2.

TS	State	Employer Name, City, State	Federal Tax Withheld	Gross Wages	FICA Withheld	Medicare Tax Withheld	State Tax Withheld	Local Tax Withheld

Forms 1 and W-2

201031 10-02-92

SPREADSHEET

	A	B	C	D	E	F	G	H	I	J	K
1	Food Service Staff	Telephone	Req.	Hours							Weekly Total
2	Assistant Managers			7/3	7/4	7/5	7/6	7/7	7/8	7/9	
3	Ching, Lei	731-4483	40+	0	0	8	8	9	8	8	41
4	Diaz, Domingo	299-6372	40+	10	10	9	8	9	0	0	46
5	Luggen, Kurt	941-1141	40+	8	0	8	9	0	8	8	41
6	Suravich, Catherine	297-0776	25+	0	10	0	0	0	8	9	27
7											
8	Busers										
9	Bronsen, Edward	554-9871	20	0	7	7	6	0	0	0	20
10	Deeters, Chris	289-3891	40+	8	8	8	8	9	0	0	41
11	Franner, Sue	451-3749	25+	8	8	5	5	0	0	0	26
12	Kacachos, Juan	297-1940	40+	0	0	8	8	8	9	9	42
13	O'Brien, Bill	943-9328	20	0	0	7	8	0	0	0	15
14	Parich, Baiju	868-2974	40+	0	0	8	8	8	8	8	40
15	Simmons, Ken	553-5580	20	8	8	5	0	0	0	0	21
16	Smith, Melissa	455-8081	40+	8	8	8	8	8	0	0	40
17	Woodward, Kamisha	299-7225	30	0	0	0	5	8	8	8	29
18											
19	Chefs										
20	Abel, Harold	553-5237	40+	8	8	8	8	8	0	0	40
21	Diamantes, Joe	868-4015	40	0	8	8	8	5	8	0	37
22	Goodman, Jerome	720-6564	25	5	5	0	0	5	5	5	25
23	Lutkenhoff, Bjorn	493-3737	40+	8	5	8	8	8	0	0	37
24	Matthews, Mick	421-5026	40	0	0	8	8	8	8	8	40
25	Willis, Bob	941-4599	40+	8	8	8	0	0	8	8	40
26											
27	Food Prep										
28	Ayers, Laura	724-0362	40+	8	8	8	8	8	0	0	40
29	Cole, Montgomery	961-1127	40+	8	8	8	8	8	0	0	40
30	DeSalvo, Marcia	753-7083	30	6	8	8	8	0	0	0	30
31	Graham, Gladys	386-0976	40+	0	0	8	8	8	8	8	40
32	Kossman, Jessie	793-3291	20	8	8	0	0	0	0	5	21
33	Lai, Chu	886-0948	20	8	8	0	0	0	0	5	21
34	Mason, Allayna	352-3583	25	0	0	5	8	8	0	0	21
35	McDonald, Geoffrey	23-4685	40+	0	0	8	8	8	8	0	32
36	Rene, Karen	221-7243	40	0	8	0	8	8	8	8	40
37	Servers										
38	Albrick, Thomas	284-9018	40+	6	6	6	8	8	8	0	42
39	Andrews, James	861-4678	40+	8	8	8	6	6	8	0	44

Spreadsheet (Continued)

	A	B	C	D	E	F	G	H	I	J	K
40	**Food Service Staff**	**Telephone**	**Req.**	**Hours**							**Weekly Total**
41				7/3	7/4	7/5	7/6	7/7	7/8	7/9	
42	Aquino, Luis	724-2919	40+	8	8	8	6	6	0	0	36
43	Brown, Megan	829-4163	40+	0	0	8	8	8	8	8	40
44	Bruosta, Roberto	221-5170	20	6	6	0	0	0	0	7	19
45	Catanzaro, Andi	422-1474	20	7	6	0	0	0	0	7	20
46	Chung, Sooyun	941-5087	40	0	0	8	8	8	8	8	40
47	Devries, Stacey	321-3812	20	6	6	0	0	0	0	0	12
47	Estes, Antoine	961-9197	20	0	6	0	0	0	8	7	21
48	Farro, Michael	575-0391	40	8	8	0	0	8	8	8	40
49	Ferrara, Rebecca	474-8966	40+	0	0	8	8	8	8	8	40
50	Haas, Chad	721-2107	30	7	7	0	0	0	8	7	29
51	Kind, Tonii	323-9123	40+	8	6	0	8	8	8	0	38
52	Kopansky, Kristina	251-9452	20	0	0	7	7	0	7	0	21
53	Lawson, Daniel	445-8219	40	0	0	8	8	8	8	8	40
54	Li, Sheng	221-5740	25	7	7	6	0	0	0	5	25
55	Moores, Deushawn	556-3226	25	6	8	0	0	0	6	6	26
56	Odom, John	281-6761	40	0	0	8	8	8	8	8	40
57	Pangallo, Dion	662-9900	40+	7	7	8	8	0	6	6	42
58	Peters, Kelly	337-3338	40	0	6	8	8	8	6	0	36
59	Rajan, Shanti	751-3654	25	5	5	0	0	5	5	5	25
60	Redington, Joyce	285-0372	40+	8	0	8	8	8	8	0	40
61	Sager, Jeffrey	734-9822	40+	0	6	6	8	8	8	6	42
62	Schmidt, Leona	221-6993	20	6	0	0	6	0	6	0	18
63	Smith, Diane	671-5029	30+	7	0	8	8	7	0	0	30
64	Speers, Adam	729-8880	40	0	0	7	8	7	8	8	38
65	Taylor, Michael	634-7852	40+	8	8	0	5	7	7	7	42
66	Thomas, Latania	677-2169	40+	0	0	8	8	8	8	8	40
67	Witt, Stephanie	421-2581	30	0	0	6	6	6	6	5	29
68	Zybko, David	231-6025	25	0	0	7	7	6	0	0	20
69											
70											
71											
72											

YOUR TELEPHONE CONVERSATION WITH MRS. LAVINIER

You pick up your telephone and dial Mrs. Lavinier's number—722-0232. The telephone rings twice and a woman's voice answers, "Lavinier residence."

You: "Hello. My name is _____. I'm from the Five Stars Hotel. I'm calling for Mrs. Margaret Lavinier about the Ladies' League luncheon this Friday."

Mrs. L: "Oh, yes, this is Mrs. Lavinier. I spoke with a Ms. Marcum this morning about the changes."

You: "We appreciate your calling ahead, Mrs. Lavinier. As I mentioned I am _____, the food service manager here at Five Stars Hotel. It's our policy for me to double-check that we have everything just as you have requested so that everything will go smoothly."

Mrs. L: "Thank you. I've spent three months trying to get this luncheon together."

You: "From the information I have, it looks like you've put a lot of thought into the details. If you don't mind, I'd like to review my part of the luncheon. May I ask you some questions that involve the food service and room setup?"

Mrs. L: "I hope there aren't any problems."

You: "Not that I'm aware of, Mrs. Lavinier. I hope by reviewing the details with you that we can provide what you expected. Ms. Marcum told me you are expecting 90 instead of 75 guests. Is that correct?"

Mrs. L: "Yes, we had a few late registrations from longtime league members. I expected a few, but not 14."

You: "So 90 guests is the number of responses you received?"

Mrs. L: "Actually, we have 88, but I rounded it up to 90."

You: "That's fine. Just for your information, we always prepare enough food and space for an additional 10 guests at no additional cost."

Mrs. L: "That sounds like a good idea. By the way, I've decided to have the three officers and the guest speaker at a head table."

You: "I'll be happy to arrange that for you. Do you want a skirt on the head table? That always looks nice."

Mrs. L: "Yes. That will be lovely."

You: "Will the speaker be needing a podium and a microphone?"

Mrs. L: "Oh, no, she said she wouldn't. She walks around when she speaks and doesn't need a microphone, so neither one will be necessary, thank you."

You: "OK. I'd like to run through the rest of the setup if that's all right."

Mrs. L: "Of course."

You: "You want round tables with eight chairs, except for the head table we just added. That will have four chairs, correct?"

Mrs. L: "Yes, that's right."

You: "The tables will be topped with white cloths and pink linen napkins, and

the head table will have a white cloth skirt, correct?"

Mrs. L: "Sounds good."

You: "We'll be using the standard dishes and flatware, with two glasses, one for water and one for a soft drink, right?"

Mrs. L: "Oh, wait, we requested iced tea instead of soft drinks. Is that there somewhere?"

You: "We can take care of that. No soft drinks, but iced tea, no problem. We're moving right into the menu. Did you want both hot coffee and hot tea with dessert?"

Mrs. L: "Yes."

You: "For the main course you have requested chicken Kiev, broccoli, and baked potato with sour cream, butter, or both."

Mrs. L: "Yes. And please make sure the broccoli is steamed. I'll hear about it if it isn't."

You: "I'll write a special note to the chefs to make sure the broccoli is steamed. For the salad you've chosen an iceberg lettuce salad with a choice of peppercorn or ranch dressing."

Mrs. L: "Actually I believe I said peppercorn and French. Also, could we have oil and vinegar on the tables, just in case?"

You: "That's not a problem. I'll change the ranch to French and add oil and vinegar. And for dessert, I have baked apples with cinnamon. I've made the changes you've requested. You've planned an excellent luncheon, and I will do my best to make it happen. I'd be happy to meet with you at 11:30, before the luncheon starts, and go over any last-minute questions with you. Would that be helpful?"

Mrs. L: "I would like that. You've certainly been accommodating to our changes. I think our luncheon will turn out quite well. Thank you."

You: "You're certainly welcome, Mrs. Lavinier. I'll look forward to talking with you this Friday. Feel free to call me with any other questions. My extension is 804. Have a good day."

Mrs. L: "Thank you."

INVOICE NO. 2553

SOLD TO	SHIPPED TO
KARAS DISTRIBUTORS	" "

STREET & NO.	STREET & NO.
808 Demo Lane	" "

CITY	STATE	ZIP	CITY	STATE	ZIP
Madison	WI	12345	"	"	"

INVOICE NO. 2562

SOLD TO	SHIPPED TO
PATRIEMONT RACING, INC.	P.R., INC.

STREET & NO.	STREET & NO.
20902 Parkway Lane	20902 Parkway Lane

CITY	STATE	ZIP	CITY	STATE	ZIP
Indianapolis	IN	12345	Indianapolis	IN	12345

INVOICE NO. 2599

SOLD TO	SHIPPED TO
SPEED RACER APPAREL	SPEED RACER APPAREL

STREET & NO.	STREET & NO.
#1 Montgomery Road	#1 Montgomery Road

CITY	STATE	ZIP	CITY	STATE	ZIP
Los Angeles	CA	12345	Los Angeles	CA	12345

INVOICE

CUSTOMER'S ORDER #	SALESPERSON	TERMS	F.O.B.	DATE REQUESTED
2599	D. CRAWFORD	30 DAYS	SURFACE	ASAP

4	GRADE 2 GLOVES #2000 (500 CT. BOX)		
2	GRADE 3 GLOVES #3000 (500 CT. BOX)		

Shipping and Receiving Schedule

Date: Tuesday, May 15	Dock No. 1
Time scheduled	**Vendor**
8:00–8:45 A.M.	Load Barrington Sporting Goods
8:45–9:45 A.M.	Load McMahan
9:45–10:00 A.M.	break
10:00–10:30 A.M.	paperwork

Staff Schedule	Ladies' League luncheon
	Shift
J. Goodman	8 A.M. – 4 P.M.
G. Graham	8 A.M. – 4 P.M.
K. Rene	8 A.M. – 4 P.M.
C. Lai	10 A.M. – 4 P.M.
M. Brown	10 A.M. – 6 P.M.
S. Chung	10 A.M. – 6 P.M.
M. Farro	10 A.M. – 6 P.M.
R. Ferrara	10 A.M. – 6 P.M.
D. Lawson	10 A.M. – 6 P.M.

Speed Racer Apparel
Packing Slip

PRO RACERS, INC.
180 South 38th Street
Provo, Utah 12345
Phone (800) 555-8888
Fax (412) 777-1212

Shipping Date: May 15, 1993   Customer No: 607728

Customer Name: Speed Racer Apparel

Customer Address: 1 Montgomery Road, Los Angeles, CA 12345

Order Number: 2599   Date Requested: ASAP

Ship Via: surface   Packed by:

Quantity	Item No.	Description of Shipment
4	2000	grade 2 gloves (500 count box)
2	3000	grade 3 gloves (500 count box)

Patriemont Racing, Inc.
Packing Slip

PRO RACERS, INC.
180 South 38th Street
Provo, Utah 12345
Phone (800) 555-8888
Fax (412) 777-1212

Shipping Date: May 15, 1993   Customer No: 607435

Customer Name: Patriemont Racing, Inc.

Customer Address: 20902 Parkway Lane, Indianapolis, IN 12345

Order Number: 2562   Date Requested: May 25, 1993

Ship Via: UPS   Packed by:

Quantity	Item No.	Description of Shipment
1	2000	grade 2 gloves (500 count box)
2	550	retardant body suits (300 count box)

TOOLBOX

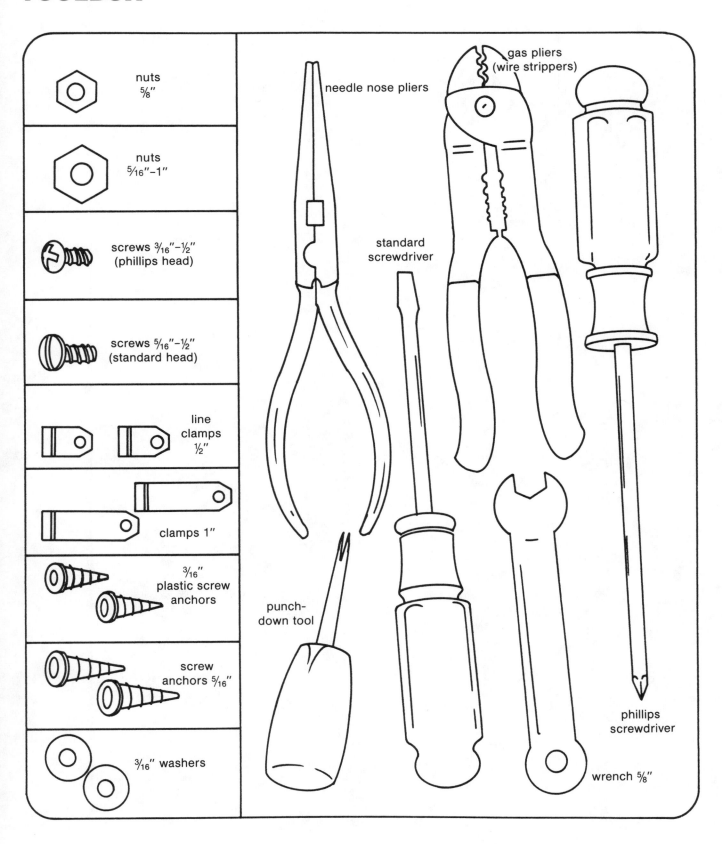

nuts
5/8"

nuts
5/16"–1"

screws 3/16"–1/2"
(phillips head)

screws 5/16"–1/2"
(standard head)

line
clamps
1/2"

clamps 1"

3/16"
plastic screw
anchors

screw
anchors 5/16"

3/16" washers

needle nose pliers

gas pliers
(wire strippers)

standard
screwdriver

punch-
down tool

phillips
screwdriver

wrench 5/8"

OPERATOR'S CODES

AACS:	All access
ACS:	Access
BP:	Binding post
CA:	Cable
CSTR:	Customer
FX:	Fax
GRP:	Group
ICPE:	Customer provided equipment
I1:	Installment instruction code
IF1:	In facilities one
IF2:	In facilities two
IF3:	In facilities three
ILA:	Identification line for address
ILN:	Identification line for name
ILOC:	Additional customer location information
INST:	Instructions
INSTL:	Install
INTL:	Initial installation
MSTR:	Master
MTNG:	Meeting
N:	On
ND:	And
OFST:	Off-site
ONST:	On-site
ORDN:	Order number
PR:	Pair
RTT:	Rotate
RMKS:	Remark(s)—displayed with limited vowels or repeat consonants
TEA:	Terminal
TN:	Telephone number
TTB:	Touch-tone base
1FB:	1 private business line
1FR:	1 private residence line

TOOLS LIST

SCREWDRIVERS
Various types and sizes
Match screwdriver tip with screw head slot

PLIERS
6-inch diagonal—cutting wire and stripping insulation
Needlenose—pulling, holding, and wrapping wires
Lineman's—cutting heavier gauge wire
Gas—pulling sheath off of different types of cable

DRILLS
Electric—drills holes in all kinds of material with right kind of bit
Yankee or Push Drill—drills pilot holes in wood or light material
Star Drill—drills small holes in masonry
Brace—drills holes in wood and other wall and floor-type construction material, ratchets
Bits—various types and sizes

WRENCHES
Lineman's—fits 3/8-, 1/2-, 5/8-, and 3/4-inch nuts with oval hole for removing pole steps
Adjustable—fits various sizes of nuts
216 Tool—fits 3/8- and 7/16-inch nuts on various field equipment
Combination—9/16-inch box end and 9/16-inch open end used in conjunction with air impact wrench
Socket Wrench—3/18-, 1/2-, 7/16-, and 9/16-inch sockets, extensions, and a variety of Allen wrench sizes, used in a variety of applications (e.g., placing and removing nuts and bolts on splice cases)
Air Impact Wrench—uses various sizes of sockets to place and remove nuts and bolts
Torque—torque nuts in inch pounds on splice cases

HAMMERS
Drilling—1 1/4-pound used with ramset or stardrill
Claw—driving and removing nails
Stepping—a small shorthand sledge hammer; 4-pound is used to place drive hooks in
Tack—driving very small nails and ground wire nails

GOGGLES
Plastic—dust and flying or falling objects
Regular Impact—flying objects only

FLASHLIGHT
replace bulbs and batteries

CABLE CUTTERS
Small—used to cut house cables up to 200pr.
Medium—used to cut cables up to 300pr.
Large—used to cut cables up to 3600pr.

SAWS
Keyhole—used to cut holes in drywall
Hacksaw—used to cut metal
Hand Pruning Saw—used to trim larger limbs on trees
Pole Pruning Saw—used with tree trimming, 6-foot section poles to reach limbs and cut off from the ground

FILES
for sharpening drill bits and splicer knife

HONING STONE
used to sharpen climbers and splicer knife

HAND TEST SET OR BUTT-SET
used to detect dial tone, check polarity of line, monitor a line, dial a number and talk

BUZZERS OR BEEPERS

provide tone to identify wires or cables, talk battery for talk wires, test for correct polarity

PROBE

used with hand test set to hear and locate tone produced by buzzer

DROP WIRE SPLITTER

splits single pair aerial drop, 2pr. and 5pr. buried drop

STAPLE GUN

fastens inside wire and other round cable and wire

D-IMPACT TOOL PUNCH-DOWN TOOL

punches wires down on various types of connectors without prestripping insulation, using a variety of interchangeable bits

PIC-A-BOND

used to splice wires together, works on 26, 24, 22, and 19 cables and inside wire

WIRE RAISING TOOL

used with 6-foot tree trimming poles to lift drop wire into place through trees

SOLDERING IRON

used to make and remove solder connections

TREE PRUNERS

used with 6-foot poles that can be connected together to reach small tree limbs 6 feet to 24 feet from ground to clear path for drop wires and telephone cables

WASHER CUTTER

used to cut circles out of hard plastic to be used when putting together splice cases

CHIPPING KNIFE

used to remove sheath from lead cables

CHIPPING BRUSH

used to roughen up sheath on plastic- and lead- covered cables to prepare them for various splicing applications

TAB CUTTERS

used to cut slits or tabs in cable sheath so cables can be properly bonded and grounded

SHAVE HOOK

used to prepare lead sheath on cables for soldering

SNIPS

used for cutting tape, muslin, and small gauge wire, and removing insulation

SPLICERS KNIFE

a very sharp knife for cutting plastic sheath, steel, and aluminum armour under sheath on various styles and sizes of cables

COLOR WHEEL AND COLOR CODE

learn Bell System color code; wheel helps to identify color of a pair given the number, e.g., Pair #1 = White Blue; Pair #2 = White Orange

AGENDA

Time (mins.)	Time period	Subject
(30)	8:00–8:30	Continental breakfast
( )	_____	_____
( )	_____	_____
( )	_____	_____
( )	_____	_____
( )	_____	_____
( )	_____	_____
( )	_____	_____
( )	_____	_____
( )	_____	_____
( )	_____	_____
( )	_____	_____
( )	_____	_____
( )	_____	_____
( )	_____	_____
( )	_____	_____
( )	_____	_____
( )	_____	_____
( )	_____	_____
( )	_____	_____
( )	_____	_____
( )	_____	_____
( )	_____	_____
( )	_____	_____
( )	_____	_____
( )	_____	_____
( )	_____	_____
( )	_____	_____

EXPENSE REPORT

TRIP

Date	Breakfast	Lunch	Dinner	Phone	Amount
Totals					

OTHER EXPENSES (Standard forms or receipts must be attached to receive reimbursement)

Mileage × .25 _____

Hotel/Motel _____

Cab Fare/Rental Car _____

Tolls _____

Parking _____

Airline Tickets _____

Micellaneous _____

Total Expenses _____

Less Advance _____

Amount Due Employee _____

I request and hereby authorize that the amount be disbursed in the following manner:

1. Payroll _____   Employee's Signature

2. Cash Payment _____   _____

3. Other (specify) _____   Supervisor's Signature

_____

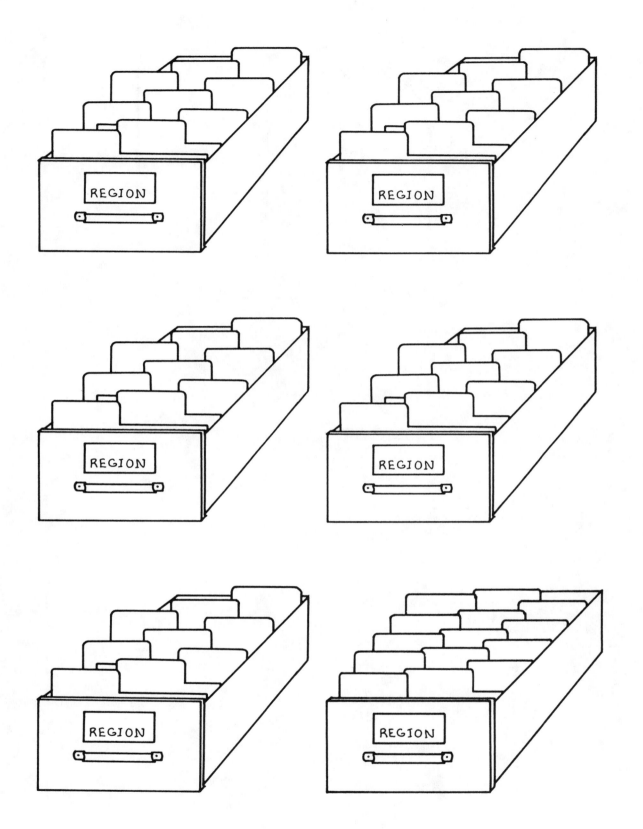